How sweet it is! Shero lives every Canadian boy's dream by sipping champagne from the Stanley Cup after the Flyers' thrilling victory over the Boston Bruins.

Shero seldom shows his emotions during the course of a game. Here he follows the action from behind the bench during a Flyers-Islanders Stanley Cup semi-final playoff game.

Shero calls instructions to a Flyer player on the bench as the hairy trio of Don Saleski, Dave Schultz and Orest Kindrachuk follow the play. Those three linemates pledged not to shave until all three had scored a goal. As of this writing, Schultz and Saleski had scored, but "Little O" was still waiting to break the ice. Such togetherness is typical of Shero's Flyers, and most observers feel their team spirit is unique in all of professional sports. Bob Kelly is at far left, Gary Dornhoefer at far right.

Beginning of a goal. Flyers power play is set up with Andre Dupont at right point, Reggie Leach in the slot and Bobby Clarke at corner of crease. With puck behind net, Islanders defenseman Dave Lewis attempts to move Clarke from in front of goalie Billy Smith. Flyers' Jimmy Watson is out of picture, working for puck in corner.

Score! Leach fires a wrist shot high over Smith's glove hand into top corner of net as Lewis sprawls in front. Play developed as Watson passed to Leach from behind net. Note Clarke's position for possible rebound.

(*Opposite*) Andre "Moose" Dupont, favorite of Spectrum fans and longtime Shero protege. Under Shero's teaching, Dupont has matured into one of the league's outstanding young defensemen. Shero also coached Dupont during their minor league days in the Rangers system. (*Below*) Shero, Tom Fowler and Bing Jackson, all stars of the Navy team that won the Manitoba championship in 1944.

Sleep well, Canada; your Navy is standing guard. Shero cuts a dashing figure as a member of Her Majesty's Navy, Winnipeg, 1944.

Shero in Winnipeg, 1949. After six years in pro hockey, he shows off his only mode of transportation.

Shero at age 20, a tough, young defenseman for the New York Rovers.

(*Opposite*) Signing autographs outside Madison Square Garden, 1947. (*Below*) Shero with friends of Jack Gordon, now general manager of Minnesota Northstars, in New York, 1946. Shero, a long time friend of Gordon, was outspoken in his defense when Gordon was criticized and replaced as coach of Minnesota several years ago.

(Above) Shero with assistants Nykoluk and Ashbee. Ashbee joined the Flyer's coaching staff after his tragic eye injury during last years' playoffs. The injury ended his playing career, but not his contributions to the team. Ashbee is credited with much of the improvement of the Flyer's young defensemen, like Watson, Bladon, Dupont and Goodenough. The Flyers staged a "Night" for Ashbee in March, one of the class events of the year. *(Opposite)* A good manager recognizes talent. Here Keith Allen, Flyers' general manager, demonstrates his recognition of a remarkable coach by lighting Shero's cigar with his old contract. The cigar celebrated Shero's new contract with the Flyers, an event greeted with great relief by the Philadelphia sporting community. There had been rumors that Shero would leave the Flyers for a fabulous offer from the WHA Minnesota Fighting Saints. Thank Heavens for all of us that he turned them down!

The Shero family: Fred with wife Mariette, sons Reajan and Jean-Paul.

Shero at home with wife, Mariette.

Shero at work at dining room table. Those who know him tell of his incessant doodling of game situations and play diagrams, always looking to improve "The System."

Shero

Shero
The Man Behind the System

By
FRED SHERO
in cooperation with
VIJAY S. KOTHARE
Introduction by
BERNIE PARENT

Chilton Book Company
RADNOR, PENNSYLVANIA

Copyright © 1975 by Fred Shero Hockey Programs, Inc.
First Edition   All Rights Reserved
Published in Radnor, Pa., by Chilton Book Company
and simultaneously in Don Mills, Ont., Canada, by
Thomas Nelson & Sons, Ltd.
Designed by Carole L. DeCrescenzo
Manufactured in the United States of America
ISBN: 0-8019-6435-0
Library of Congress Catalog Card Number: 75-15018
Photos courtesy of Philadelphia Flyers, Inc.,
Vijay S. Kothare, and Martin W. Kane.
Captions by Robert Norman Boucher

I dedicate this book to my family, but especially to my children since they don't know me. I hope that after reading the book, they will finally get to know and understand me.

Fred Shero

Contents

Introduction by Bernie Parent, 9
Chapter 1 *Early Life,* **13**
Chapter 2 *Hardships and Fun,* **23**
Chapter 3 *Help from a Friend,* **37**
Chapter 4 *Life as a Professional Athlete,* **51**
Chapter 5 *Violence in Hockey,* **59**
Chapter 6 *Some Training Techniques,* **77**
Chapter 7 *Thoughts on Coaching,* **87**
Chapter 8 *Inside the Flyers' System,* **101**
Chapter 9 *What's the Future for Hockey?* **111**
Chapter 10 *Predictably Unpredictable,* **117**
Coaching Chart, 139

Introduction

Right now, we, the Philadelphia Flyers, have the greatest hockey team in the world.

Why?

One reason, we have a great collection of players. But, players alone do not win hockey games.

In a lot of ways, a hockey team is like a machine. You have the best machine in the world with all the best parts, but you still need a skilled man to operate the machine or it will not do the job it is intended to do. Our hockey team has all the best parts. But it would not perform the way it does if it did not have a skilled man running it. And, there's no one in hockey with more skill than Fred Shero.

Freddie's got a way of handling players. He seems to know just what to do and say in every situation.

A lot of times we do not understand Freddie, but we believe in him. So, if he says something, we do it. We know he has a reason for everything he tells us and no one can argue with his record.

I know that Freddie has made me a success both in sports and in life. He has made me think and realize a lot more things than I did before.

I think everyone on the team owes Freddie a lot. I know I do.

Bernie Parent

Shero

chapter 1

Early Life

I could hear the familiar cries and shouts as distinctly as the pounding of my heart.

"Pass the puck," shouted the center.

"Watch the screen," cried the goalie, "and the slot."

"Pick the left wing," cried the opposition.

"Get out of my way." Our goalie slashed the opposition's forward who was parked right in front of the nets.

I could see the pressure mounting as our team was trailing by two goals, but I couldn't do anything about it. Where was I when the team needed me?

I was helping Dad in the work shed behind the house. Just a few yards away, the game was in progress and I could see it through the small window. The boys were pushing the puck around and enjoying it.

School was already out for better than four hours, and Dad's pocketwatch was about to declare the magic hour, seven. I was helping Dad with the small chores like putting away his tools in their slots on the pegboard, tidying up the workbench and sweeping the floor. Mom was busy in the kitchen, preparing the evening meal.

It was the winter of 1934 in Winnipeg, Manitoba. I was nine. While my friends were putting in ice-time, I was knee-deep in wood shavings and sawdust covered my hair.

My interests took second place to Dad's ethics. Work came before play, even for a nine-year-old. I was always the only one who had chores while my friends had none.

Dad was a carpenter. That's what our neighbors called him. But it was difficult to put a label on this man who designed houses, remodeled rooms and created furniture. To me, he was an artist and an intellectual who loved Russian literature and music, discussed theology, studied history, counseled our neighbors and worked hard to keep the family together. As a craftsman, he used his tools with the precision and discipline of a surgeon. Patiently he would study the drawings and recreate them in his mind. No detail was too small for his trained eyes. He survived the depression because he was able to use his hands. Survival from that time on was on his mind constantly.

He never tired of sharing his knowledge, from the beauty of nature to the cross cuts in lumber. He would take me with him to the lumberyard and try to teach me the fine points of selecting the right lumber for the right job.

"Life is like carpentry," he would say. "What you get from a piece of lumber depends on the details you put into it. If you leave it to chance, chances are you won't make it."

The game of hockey is somewhat like carpentry. The plays must be honed and polished and never left to chance. It requires a system. Without it, the game lacks character. It becomes mediocre.

But on that cold October evening, the only lumber that was on my mind was the hockey stick. Suddenly I heard Mom's voice.

"Alex," she cried through the kitchen door. Oh! what a sweet voice that was—not because it belonged to Mom, but because it meant that dinner was ready.

I could smell the potatoes that were cooking in the kitchen. Dad puffed his nostrils and dusted his hands. He patted my shoulder and smiled, as if to say he was glad the day was over. His smile was catchy and his face content. Dad was a happy man, no doubt. But he rarely smiled. It seemed that he reserved that special smile for his family.

We were lucky to have a piece of meat and potatoes that evening. The depression had made everybody's life painful. The immigrant families were the hardest hit. The piece of meat on our table had come from a farmer who had paid Dad in kind, since there wasn't much cash around. Dad had built the man's barn and rebuilt his house. The potatoes came from the garden we had farmed that summer.

During the dirty thirties, as Dad referred to the depression period, the local government would allow people to rent vacant plots of land for one dollar an acre. Dad in his boundless enthusiasm had taken over a piece of ground that was the size of a football field. For a man who stood only five-feet-four, he had the energy of a giant. He never thought in terms of building one chair or planting one row of peas or renovating one corner of a room.

Every project was special for him and soon, as was to be expected, he planned rows of peas, carrots, tomatoes, hills of potatoes and many other vegetables all on paper. Every spring he would pull out his plans for the garden. He rotated the crops, left some areas fallow and put in new crops. He instructed me on the basics of agriculture. The first year was the worst, but once the ground was tilled, it became easier every year to take care of it. I don't know where he found the time to till the field, but I spent hours raking it and getting it ready to receive the seeds and the tiny tomato plants.

The weeding and water jobs were left up to me. I had to carry pails of water to the field a few blocks away; and on days when the other chores around the house were heavy, I felt I was watering the entire North American continent.

Canada is blessed with a short growing season. The fertile soil, the warm sun and my work under Dad's watchful eye brought us a hundred bushels of potatoes and mounds of tomatoes. These vegetables fed us all winter long.

Gardening kept me so busy that I had neither time nor energy to waste. It didn't take long to make the garden into my private world. Here I watched nature at work, and I soon realized that nature had a system. If I didn't water or weed the garden, the results were disastrous. As a child I was told that nature played no favorites, yet it appeared the weeds were growing faster than the peas and carrots. Couldn't nature have put all its energy into my peas and carrots rather than distributing some to the weeds?

"Nature is a great teacher," Dad would say,

"man learns from it, but he also makes a few changes. Sometimes we try to make nature more livable. If only Mother Nature could speak out, she would give man a pat on the back. But other times? Like war, Freddie, who is to say that this man is a weed and must be destroyed?"

Dad's love had no limits. If fate had been kinder to him, he would have been a Schweitzer or a Gandhi. Although fate made him small in stature, his enthusiasm and affection were boundless.

In fact, it was Dad's generosity that put vegetables on many of our neighbors' plates during the dirty thirties. Yet none bothered to help me weed and water the field. They would see me going back and forth with pails of water. Sometimes, I would work from seven in the morning to seven at night. Mom would come along to weed and my two little sisters played hopscotch in the rows. But there were no signs of the neighbors.

Dad held up the sports page for me to see the picture of Max Baer, who had knocked out Primo Carnera early that year in New York.

"Be a boxer," he hinted as he looked at me.

But my mind was on the game that was in progress not too far from the house. I was hoping to make the team at the Lord Nelson School. Our coach had shown interest in my stick handling and had told me to get more ice-time. An hour a day wasn't enough, he told me. But that's all the time I had, so I had to squeeze four hours of practice into one hour of play.

"There's no future for hockey players," Dad said seriously, trying to draw my attention.

"Alex, let the boy finish his meal," Mom said softly. It was her way of telling Dad that this wasn't the time to talk about my future.

Mom was small in height, but hardly tiny. Dad had married her when she was seventeen. He was in his early twenties. A year later, they fled from Russia and immigrated to Canada. Mom often talked about the white stallion her family had given Dad as her dowry when they got married in Saratov, a town on the Volga River in the heartland of Russia. "White like pure snow," she used to say. She must have loved that horse.

But the stallion had to stay behind when they decided to leave Russia rather suddenly. Dad had taken objection to his father's continued mistreatment of his mother. In his anger, Dad hit his own father and soon after had to leave Russia. With two sacks full of clothes and loaves of bread, they sailed for Canada and landed in Halifax, where they were told of a community of Russian immigrants in Winnipeg.

"Hockey players have no future."
The words were ringing through my head

as I tried to devour the potatoes and gravy. The images of Harvey Jackson and Charles Conacher flashed through my mind.

"No future?" I asked myself. At age nine, future to me was the next weekend, a time of fun and games. I never realized what Dad was saying until much later.

Hockey as a profession had no future in those days, and those who did reach the major leagues were blessed with a love for the game. Most people looked upon hockey players as bums, because their income never kept up with their enthusiasm or their sweat. Professional hockey in my Dad's mind was not enough for me, especially since I got good grades in school.

Since Dad had left Russia at an early age, he never did get a chance to finish his education. Survival required a trade and he turned to carpentry. His life had been a sad game of catch-up, of trying to keep ahead of poverty and hardships. He was a practical man, though, and always reminded us not to commit the mistakes he had made.

My older brothers, unfortunately, never showed much ambition. They disappointed Dad, but somehow he knew their limitations and allowed them to lead their own lives. One brother became a carpenter, and the others merely drifted away. If any one of them were to cross my path today, I wouldn't know what to say to them.

My older brothers were more than nine years my senior, so I suspect my arrival was quite a surprise to my parents. Therefore, Dad took a greater interest in my education and future.

"Emily," Dad muttered as he turned to Mom and looked at her through his tiny spectacles. He shook his head as if to say, "Don't interrupt me when I'm trying to put some sense into the only boy who shows some promise of making something out of himself."

"Do you know what a hockey player does after thirty-five?" he inquired. Dad's voice was firm but gentle. My sisters nudged me under the table and Mom wrinkled her face.

"Nothing, absolutely nothing. He's out of a job and has to look for a new one," Dad said as he threw his hands in the air. "Freddie, get an education. Become a doctor."

There was a knock on the kitchen door and Jim Mosienko appeared at the window waving his stick. Dad looked at my face and nodded approvingly. I darted out with my hand-me-down skates and made for the rink.

chapter 2
Hardships and Fun

My parents were unconcerned about my interest in sports. To them it was just a safety-valve that released my energies. We needed safety-valves that didn't get us into trouble.

"Better this than thieving," Mom often said as she cleaned my scraped knees, bruised shins and chin and applied homemade remedies to keep the wounds from infection.

Poor neighborhoods breed problem kids and gangs. Our neighborhood was no different. I could have become a problem child just by associating with the wrong crowd. But by the time I was through with chores for Mom around the house and chores for Dad in the work shed and basement, I didn't have enough time to play hockey, much less the time to spend with the guys.

Even on Saturdays, I had to accompany my father to the lumberyard or job-site where he was either building a new house or patching up an old one. While he carried the heavy tool kit, I followed him like his shadow. Since we had no car, the journey started soon after breakfast. We had to walk three miles in the cold to the trolley-stop and wait for the trolley to show up.

The trolley would begin its slow journey, and it seemed to go everywhere except where we were supposed to go. My impatience always made Dad smile, and he would talk to me just to calm me down. My childish mind felt that there was some conspiracy to keep me from playing hockey on Saturday mornings, while all the other kids were already out in the streets with their sticks.

We lived in the Russian section of Winnipeg, because it was a social necessity. The neighborhood was made up of Polish, Russian and German immigrants, whose instincts for survival were stronger than their knowledge of English, French or the Canadian lifestyle. Here my parents felt secure. Living among the folks from the old country made it easy for Mom and Dad to adjust to a foreign lifestyle.

"This is English country," Dad would often begin his lectures on the problems of the neighborhood. "The only way a Russian immigrant's son will make good is for him to be better."

Obviously, he meant better than the English. Being better was not easy. To make one's mark in the world, one needed a college education. The poor immigrant parents didn't have the money to send their children to college. My father barely made enough to take care of his family. There were no jobs in Canada during the dirty thirties. People who were fortunate enough to have jobs worked long hours. Many evenings after putting in a ten to sixteen-hour day, my father would be too tired even to listen to his favorite program of Russian music that played on a local radio station.

The boys of these working immigrants, therefore, either played sports to occupy their time or they joined gangs. I don't even know what the girls did in those days. In most cases, parents didn't care what their kids did in their spare time and most boys were left to their own devices. Those of us who wanted to read books couldn't go to the library, because the nearest library was six miles away.

In other words, we had no cultural heritage.

Our parents' culture and way of life didn't interest us. Their dreams and mannerisms were old-fashioned. If we tried to be like the English or French people who lived in the more affluent neighborhoods, our parents would frown. This hatred between the European immigrants and the second or third generation French and English continued even after we grew up. There was always the feeling of superiority among the English and French communities. The immigrants were always the lowest on the totem pole. Even attempts by the younger generation to rise above the ethnic barriers were frowned upon by the older generation. If a girl from our neighborhood dated an English boy, for instance, she was called frivolous by her people, while the boy's parents mistreated her as they would an animal. I remember the time when one of my sisters was dating an English boy. Mom was furious and asked me to find out all I could about the boy and even try to keep him from seeing my sister. The boy's parents had similar ideas. I told Mom that they loved each other. To me that was all that mattered.

Even when I met my wife, I had to fight the old system. I was thirty-one then and player-coach of the hockey club in Shawinigan, which is 90 miles north of Montreal. Winnipeg was over 2,000 miles away. I was going by a drug store one Saturday morning in Shawinigan, and there I saw her behind the counter. I walked in and took a good look and said to myself, "She doesn't know it yet, but she is going to be my wife."

I walked up to her and tried to carry on a conversation, but she appeared nervous. But she knew who I was. She had seen me walk by the store many times. I guess it helped being a player-coach of the only hockey club in town. After our first date, I said, "Let's get married."

Her parents said, "What about courtship!"

Courtship? I didn't have the time. The season was about over and I was returning to Winnipeg. I had made my decision that I wanted to marry her. I told her father that I'd court her after we were married. In those days courtships lasted for months. I couldn't convince him that we were old enough to know what we were doing. He stood his ground. Besides, her family was French. I think my hockey reputation helped to overcome racial objections.

The season was over and I drove over 2,000 miles home to Winnipeg. I told Mom about Marietta, and she didn't mind if I married a French girl. I got in the car and drove the same 2,000 miles back to Shawinigan. I said, "It's now or never." Her father thought my behavior was quite romantic.

In our neighborhood there was neither a

library nor a gymnasium. The gymnasium was seven miles away in the better section of town. Many of the boys turned to crime in a small way to keep body and soul together. If a kid was not seen on the streets for six months, the neighbors figured he was in jail. That's what the neighbors thought when I came home after playing for the New York Rangers. Some even asked me what I had done to be in jail.

During the dirty thirties, there was nobody around to teach us the fine points of the game. Television and instant replays were not around then to show us the techniques of Rocket Richard, Harvey Jackson or Charlie Conacher. Sometimes we walked miles to a theater to see a few minutes of news film about a pro game. Most of our hockey news came from the local newspaper. A few photos would show the results of a hip-check or a defenseman on the ice, blocking a shot, or other action; but how much can one learn from pictures showing players frozen in mid-air? Such pictures were a credit to the photographers, but did little to show us how the plays were executed.

In those days, there were no books or clinics to teach us how to play goal or defense or forward. So we picked up the game by instinct. I suppose even the professionals played by instinct. But they had the advantage of watching the better players on their team and the opposing teams. Having gone through the baptism of professional sports, I know that it takes a special instinct to hone one's talents. Without that instinct, one never learns to outsmart the opposition or take advantage of its mistakes. Without that instinct, a hockey player can't excel at the game.

But as kids, we wanted to have fun. Proper equipment or not, it made little difference in our enjoyment of the game. Even when we faced a team from the better neighborhoods, we never felt inferior. Some of the boys, whose families were well-to-do, would strut into the makeshift rink loaded down with some expensive equipment.

Their unscarred shins were protected by shin pads, and gloves covering their hands were like barn doors. The goalie looked really silly with all those heavy pads which slowed down his movements. When he went down, he couldn't quite get up fast enough to handle a rebound.

The rich kids usually came into our neighborhood to show off their equipment. If their snobbish parents had ever found out where their children were, these boys would have gotten a licking. Instead, we licked them. They couldn't figure out how we could play hockey without pads and gloves, and some of us even played without skates. If expensive equipment guaranteed victories, then they had us over a barrel. But equipment doesn't make a team superior.

The rich kids, as we called them, lacked something. They didn't have a hard life. To us, however, hardship was a way of life, and we had the instinct to survive. They were probably shielded from the depression and maybe became doctors, lawyers and professors, while we were marked for the factories and menial trades.

We made up for our lack of equipment with a tough attitude. It was our mind over their slashing sticks. Actually our mind was on the game and not on the little cuts and bruises on our unprotected shins.

Sometimes we rolled newspapers around our legs to protect our shins. Some of us even stuffed our shirts with sheets of newspapers, but such paper-protection didn't stay in place and had to be thrown away. We wore mittens instead of gloves, but they froze in the minus-twenty-degree weather.

Some of the boys played without skates, while there were others who had no sticks. They just kicked the puck around. This is a good exercise for those who are learning to play hockey.

Instinct to hang on and the desire to excel are great qualities, and all successful people have them. But those who get carried away with success and make life unbearable for those around them should remember that there is a lighter side to life. Life has to be fun, if one can find it. As kids, we knew how to have fun, even when our shins were bleeding and our knuckles were cracked.

The trouble with most professional sports is that the fun has gone out of them. Sports has to be fun even at the professional level. Perhaps more so. A professional athlete's life is brief to begin with. If he can't have fun while playing the sport, what good is it? Instances of drugs and other artificial stimulants in professional sports do not speak well for athletes. Life is hard enough without having to make it harder.

A professional team can't be expected to produce beyond its capabilities. Constant pressures by management, press or fans will not change a team's performance. The public doesn't realize that a professional athlete is human. He has emotions and feelings, and also has a personal life. He makes mistakes just like everybody else. Some of them are glaring mistakes. It amuses me when sportscasters try to belittle athletes by making nasty comments about their mistakes as if they were experts. It is easy to criticize from the sportscasters' booth.

But when we were children, there were no

pressures of criticism from hostile commentators or sportswriters. We were out to have fun.

One of the less traveled back streets was converted into a rink. Our first job was to scrape away the surface and pile the ice like a dike around the rink. This scraping not only gave us a smooth ice surface, but it also removed the particles of black soot and small chunks of coal that flew from the surrounding chimneys. The chunks of coal often caused holes in the surface that were dangerous for skaters.

Sides were marked off and garbage cans were brought in from obliging neighbors to serve as goal posts. They were filled to the brim with snow to make them stable.

The dike-like structure around the rink served as our boards and was supposed to stop the puck from leaving the ice. But this was a little too much to expect from a foot-high pile of snow, which was always trampled over by our five to eight-year-old fans who wanted to sneak on the ice and take part in the game.

The game always started with a shaven tennis ball that was frozen so it wouldn't bounce. But it never lasted. How can one expect a frozen ball to last under the constant hitting and kicking of the rowdy bunch of boys? It would shatter like heavy pottery, and then we would kick its broken pieces until they were lost.

"Let's get a puck. I've got 10 cents," someone would say.

A rubber puck cost 25 cents, and that was a lot of money in those days. In fact, for some people it would be an hour's wage. We would all run home and return with a few cents. I never got an allowance for helping Dad, so my few cents came from Mom who got them from a glass jar. I always thought that she had kept those cents and nickels in the jar for just such an occasion.

There was another glass jar that was always on our minds. This one was in a local grocery store, and it stood behind the counter in full view with its inventory of rubber pucks. Some of the boys were always making plans to steal the jar. I wished for those pucks to just roll away in my direction. Playing with a rubber puck was a luxury; and since we were able to have fun without luxuries, we could do without a puck.

As a clever substitute, a few boys once slipped in a wooden disk that was painted black to resemble a rubber puck. Those who made the wooden puck thought it was funny, but it hurt a lot of us, particularly the little kids who came to watch us play.

As the game progressed, chunks of the snow that served as our boards would disappear. Our little fans would cart the snow away to make snowmen. There was plenty of snow around for them to play with, but they had to take away our boards. Then snowball fights, which often spilled over into the play-area, would start among the fans along the sidelines.

Although the snow piles served as temporary barriers, they failed to hold the fans out or the pucks in. The pucks or their substitutes, and we had many, flew out as if they had wings, never to be recovered. A game of ice hockey could not proceed without a puck, be it of rubber, a shaven tennis ball or horse manure.

No historian of the game has ever recorded when the first kid came up with a ready solution for a recurring problem. The problem was obvious, trying to find a puck. The horse was the answer.

Historians have often talked about a horse's role in man's progress through the centuries. They tell us that a horse has given man considerable mobility, both in war and in commerce. Over the years, many statues of horses have been raised. But these horses only anchor generals, noblemen and politicians. Not once have I seen a memorial to a horse for his service to sports.

If such a memorial exists, it is usually to honor the animal's contributions to horse racing —gambling to be precise. A memorial that is raised by those callous odds-makers who measure the animal's worth by its winnings or its stud fees.

As kids, we were quite aware of a horse's

role in our hockey games, but cared little for its role in history. On Saturdays, horses appeared on the streets pulling big delivery wagons that brought the week's supply of cheese, vegetables, meat and dry goods to stock the stores.

We took turns trailing the wagons. It seemed to us the animals knew what we were after. I often marveled at their instinct to drop exact portions that we could shape into pucks. I don't remember trailing one that had irregularity. Even if it did, the below-freezing weather froze all exposed matter. The stuff had to be manageable if it was to withstand a melee of sticks and skates.

Under a severe impact, these flattened cakes of horse manure came whizzing through the cold air like some unearthly projectiles. When they shattered, we ducked and closed our gaping mouths for fear of taking in the flying fragments. I have taken a few of those pucks right on the mouth, and it was part of the game we were playing. There was no humiliation in chasing horses and picking manure. And it didn't matter how many of those pucks we smashed, because there were always enough to go around.

chapter 3

Help from a Friend

Jim Mosienko sat on the steps of our house one evening, scratching his lean cheeks. He crossed one leg over the other, shifted his body and stroked his arms to brace against the cold. Suddenly he dropped his right leg, winced a little and grabbed his calf.

"Still stiff from last night?"

He nodded as he ran his fingers over the calf, trying to force circulation through the stiffened muscle. He tossed his head, slapped the calf and smiled.

"Tomorrow we're going for the tryouts," he said calmly.

"We?" I inquired.

"I'll be fine."

"Yeah, you'll be fine, even with that stiff leg. I don't think I can make it."

"Afraid of the big boys," he muttered half in jest, but it hit me like an insult. I have never been afraid of anything in my life. But the thought of going to the tryouts brought on the same cold chills as when Mom took me to school on the first day.

"That'll be fine," I said, "you and me on the same team."

Jim and I were the same age, but he was one of those rare natural athletes who seemed to do everything without effort. At the age of twelve, he was considered the best athlete in town. As a kid, I never thought of making it to the majors. Jim and I had played around on ice for years. We also played in the playground league when we were nine and ten. One year our team won the playground championship of Manitoba. I think that was my first thrill in life. A banquet was held in our honor and we each got a copper penny with a picture of a hockey player on it. Winning the playground championship would be the same as winning the intermediate division championship in baseball today.

After the playground league came the juvenile and junior leagues. Then came the professional leagues. The time had come for Jim and me to try for the juvenile leagues. But competition was tough. Boys came from all over town to try out at the arena. I knew I was good, but there were many others who were equally good and even better than I.

"What chance have I got of making a team?" I asked Jim.

"You gotta have confidence," Jim said and laughed.

Suddenly, he turned around and wished my father a good evening as Dad came up the walk.

"What's with Jimmy's leg?" Dad asked. "Whatever it is, he'll get over it." Dad disappeared into the house.

"Did ya hear that?" Jim smiled. "Your Dad has confidence in me. You know why? Because I've confidence in me."

"C'mon, Jim, he knows you. You're pretending about that leg, aren't you?"

"Ha, I almost got ya. Don't be so trusting all the time," said Jim as if he were making a mental note to himself about my well-being.

Very early in our lives, Jim had taken on the task of being my friend. Our friendship grew as hockey became a passion for both of us. But with Jim, hockey was more than a passion. It had become a lifestyle. He had pushed all other interests aside, including his school work. I helped him with his studies and he appreciated that. I admired his boldness and felt comfortable in his company because he gave me confidence. Without his confidence in my abilities, I would never have become a professional hockey player. He gave me the push that eventually led me to the major leagues.

Suddenly a big snowball came through the air and crashed on Jim's head. Before he could recover from the shock, another snowball and still another came crashing down on him. Finally, he turned around to brace himself from another attack.

A pink face with dirty blond locks appeared from behind the lilac tree my father had planted. When the figure of Walt Gasek appeared in full view, Jim swiftly arched his arm like a pitcher releasing a fastball and hit Walt with a snowball.

"You clown," Walt shouted. "You may be the best athlete in all of Winnipeg, but you gotta learn about snowball fights."

Jim narrowed his eyes and flung his arms around Walt as they came over to the step and sat down beside me.

"What was all that hobbling?"

"I was testing Freddie," Jim muttered.

"If you think you're rehearsing for a school play, you'd be a flop," rejoined Walt.

"School play? That's for ya scholars. Ya're a good hockey player, Walt, but guess where ya're going to end up. A professor some place.

Those books are going to bury ya. Now here's a man unto my heart. Freddie, here, is coming with me to the tryouts tomorrow. Ya can come too, and I can get ya in," Jim remarked with authority.

"No chance," Walt murmured in a low voice. "Papa won't let me. If he ever caught me playing hockey with you fellows, he'd whip me."

"Is that why ya hide the equipment in Freddie's house?"

Walt enjoyed hockey, but he always had his stick and gloves in our house. None of the boys knew how Walt's father felt about professional hockey players. He held them in as low regard as my father did.

Walt's father, also an immigrant, had decided to give his children a good education from the start. I don't even know how he managed it. His financial means were in no way superior to my father's. He worked hard and denied his wife and himself even the smallest pleasures so that Walt and his sister could get an education.

Walt studied diligently to please his father and came to like it. He also played hockey with us whenever he could and became a fine hockey player.

Jim had realized that his remark had hurt Walt.

"Don't worry," he whispered. "It'll be our secret. Nobody will know about it ever."

"I hope Papa doesn't find out about hiding

my equipment with Freddie," Walt said in a voice meant for prayer.

"I bet your father already knows," observed Jim. As he saw the color drain from Walt's face, he added. "But he respects ya for obeying him. Have ya considered that?"

"I just don't understand Papa," Walt tried to sum up his childhood in one sentence.

"Don't try to understand him, enjoy him," Jim blurted philosophically. "He is not around for ever. The little tree grows up into a big tree and tries to reach the moon. . . ." Jim spread his arms into the slate sky and looked like a big tree.

"Bravo," came a voice over our heads. My father was standing behind us.

"What're ya boys planning to do?" my father asked. "No game going on up the street?"

"The street lights aren't working, and we can't play in the dark," Walt answered. "Papa says there's not enough electricity coming into this part of town because a generator is broken."

"This time it's the generator, aye, Walt!"

"Yes, Sir.' Walt tried to explain how electricity was generated.

"Here's one smart boy, like Freddie." Father patted us and went into the house.

We all laughed at Jim who turned around and took a bow. His antics had amused Walt, who was suggesting ways to spend the evening since the hockey game was called off. Jim suggested a walk into town to see a movie, but I was too tired to make a roundtrip of fourteen miles in the deep snow. Besides I couldn't stay up late during weekdays.

"Let's roast some potatoes," said Walt, "I'm kind of hungry anyway."

"I'll start the fire,' muttered Jim as I went to the basement to get a pail of potatoes.

When I returned, they had gathered a few pine logs and boughs. Jim made a shallow depression in the snow and piled up the wood for our fire. I lifted a live coal from the fireplace in the house and put it on the boughs, and before long we had a roaring, crackling fire. Walt buried the potatoes in the coals and the three of us sat down by the fire and talked about the tryout until the potatoes were cooked.

The day of the tryouts had arrived. It was perhaps the most important day in my life. Yet, it seemed no different from all the others. Through the upstairs window, I could see the half-burned logs from our bonfire. The sun was still below the horizon even though the school bell was due to ring in an hour.

In the darkness, I could hear the sounds of day rolling up the street. The women were out with their brooms, clearing away the snow from their front steps. The horse-drawn wagons were passing by the house. A few dogs were barking. The hoot owl, nestling in the distance, let out its last hoot before retiring for the day.

The darkened school across the yard from our house was coming to life, as pale yellow lights were turned on in the classrooms. My two little sisters were sleeping soundly in their beds.

The day began like any other, no doubt. The cycle of life would come full circle for some. To me it was a day of baptism. Somewhere out there, the high-priest of hockey was waiting to test me. I was frightened.

Hot biscuits and a bowl of porridge were waiting for me in the kitchen. But my stomach was in a knot and I could hardly keep my breakfast down.

"Are ya sick?" Dad asked as he felt my head and throat.

"Just not hungry, Dad."

"You were in the basement sharpening your skates last night," said Mom as her eyes lit up.

"Some special game tonight, ha?" Dad tried to coax an explanation out of me.

"Nothing special, Dad, Jim is taking me into town tonight for tryouts," I finally blurted out trying to make it appear that the occasion did not call for the family's concern.

"First tryouts, aye, like a bride going to her wedding," Dad said dryly as he slapped my shoulders. "If ya don't make it, the world will still be here, understand? And we'll love ya no less, right, Mom? Get that food down before it gets cold."

I don't remember what happened that day at school. I returned home, helped Mom with the chores around the house and helped Dad in the shed. After dinner, Jim Mosienko and I set out. Walt Gasek joined us on the way. The three of us, with our skates over our shoulders and sticks in our hands, set out like young knights to the arena.

The snow still lay heavy and in some spots it was almost three feet deep. As we walked with deliberate steps, doubts and fears about making the team stormed my mind.

"Have you ever been to the tryouts before?" I asked Jim, who had remained unusually quiet. He slashed his stick through the snow and without much emotion said, "No." It was a positive no, as only Jim could say it. He gave no outward sign of being nervous.

"Aren't you afraid?"

"Of what? A bunch of boys who can't play hockey? Everybody is nervous. I don't feel any different. Just watch me. Do what I do and we'll make the team." Jim's voice was reassuring.

"I wish I was trying out for the team," Walt blurted as if he had to get rid of that thought and couldn't hold it ay longer.

"We'll all try out," Jim laughed as he tapped Walt with his stick.

"What do I say if he selects me?" asked Walt.

"You'll be the first kid from our neighborhood to turn down a team."

As we passed a bar, a tipsy patron was being thrown out of the place by a burly bartender. The radio was playing loud and we could hear "O, Canada...." This meant a hockey game was about to begin in some big town, and it was quite obvious that the Toronto Maple Leafs was one of the teams.

The drunk patron was singing the praises of the Leafs, and this was no surprise. In those days everybody west of Toronto rooted for the Leafs. Radio was gaining popularity and with it the Toronto Maple Leafs. This was the only team that broadcast its games. The commentators, who were employees of the Leafs, took advantage of the air time, and over the years built up the Toronto players as the good guys.

A legal check by the opposition was labeled an assault, and minor infractions committed by the Leafs were usually referred to as freak accidents.

In those days we grew up with two assumptions. One was that the Royal Canadian Mounted Police was the best police force in the world. The other was that the Toronto Maple Leafs was the best hockey team in the world. Both were the good guys. The Mounties deserved that reputation, but not the Leafs. Toronto's radio had given the Leafs' big front line national recognition. Harvey Jackson, Charles Conacher and Primo Carnera had become Canada's sports heroes, at least in our part of town.

Everybody I grew up with wanted to identify with Jackson. He was a big man and a strong checker. According to the Toronto commentators, he dominated the ice with his skating and puck-handling skills.

Jim's one overpowering desire in life was to emulate Jackson, and he made no pretense about it.

"Jackson is the best," Jim was often heard saying as he sang the big forward's praises. Jim wasn't alone. All the kids wanted to be like Jackson, and even I wanted to be like Jackson.

"I like Primo," said Walt as we walked the lonely streets into town.

"He's not great like Jackson," Jim argued.

"Yea, but you need a pretty good center to make your wings look good," Walt fired back.

Jim couldn't quite disagree with Walt, so he turned to me for my comments.

"Why Jackson?" I asked.

"He's big," began Jim's explanation as he flexed his muscles. "He's strong, and those body checks of his. . . ." He nudged Walt a little with his shoulder and let out a howl.

"Have you seen Jackson play?" asked Walt in defense.

"Don't you listen to the radio? Those guys with the mikes always talk about his body checks and fast skating."

"I've got to see what I believe, and since I haven't seen big Jackson play, I'll not make up my mind."

"Listen to the professor, will ya," Jim remarked in fun. "Well, maybe they do talk too much, but he's still the best darn hockey player in Canada today."

"How about Conacher?" I asked.

"I like Conacher, too," said Jim. "I like all three forwards, but Jackson is my hero."

I would have expected Jim to identify with Conacher because both had older brothers who played hockey. Charlie's brother Lionel was considered the best athlete in Canada at that time. He had a respect that none of the other hockey players could muster, primarily because he was a college graduate who had made it big in professional sports. He played defense for the Leafs, and I imagine he used his training as a boxer very skillfully against the opposition. Lionel made many all-star teams. Later, he entered politics and became a Member of Parliament.

Charlie, however, was a free spirit, a maverick of sorts, just like Jim. He excelled in hockey, though, and displayed the best shot in the game. But Charlie never gained the reputation that followed Lionel through life. From professional hockey to politics was quite an outstanding achievement at a time when hockey players were generally considered to be bums.

By the time we made it to the arena, the tryouts were already in progress. Boys of all sizes and shapes had surrounded the rink, and parents were busy preparing their broods with last minute instructions. Mothers adjusted caps and scarves, tucked in shirts and wiped noses. Fathers were handing out final tips.

Our entrance was completely ignored by the crowd and I was happy to remain unnoticed. But Jim walked over to the coach who stood by the rink with his assistants. Jim grabbed the man's hand and shook it vigorously. Nobody shook the coach's hand in those days. Jim's outgoing manner had a way of reaching people. The coach, however, remained cool to Jim's behavior.

Jim laced his skates and stepped onto the ice. He had no difficulty convincing the coach that he could skate, hit the puck and shoot the nets. He was motioned off the ice and told that he had made the team.

The coach pointed in my direction and I stepped onto the ice. I went through all the drills nervously. I was not used to blank stares from the assembled boys who followed my moves.

The coach waved me off the ice with his fat finger and an unconcerned look in his eye. But the moment I saw his fat finger dismiss me as if I were a piece of carcass in a butcher shop, I resigned myself to an uneventful ending to an eventful day.

But what surprised me was Jim. Since the coach turned me down, Jim gave the thumbs down sign to the coach.

"Freddie and I come as a package. We'll play together on the same team," he insisted.

The coach looked at my scrawny figure and he had to settle for Jim's terms.

I have been grateful to Jim. Without his confidence in me, I would have never made it in hockey. There were many boys in our neighborhood who were better hockey players than I, but they never had Jim Mosienko on their side to give them confidence. As fate would have it, the high-priest of hockey had finally smiled on me as I slaved to perfect my game and was later spotted by a New York scout.

For Jim, however, the fame and romance of professional hockey never came. He never took his place beside Jackson. His brother Bill made it to the Hockey Hall of Fame. Bill was four years senior to Jim.

Walt Gasek became a good hockey player, but he never made it to the pros. He used his hockey talents to win a scholarship to the University of Michigan. Years later after Walt had graduated and become a geologist, his father confessed to me that he shouldn't have been so harsh with Walt's interest in hockey.

He said, "I guess sports and education go together after all."

chapter *4*

Life as a Professional Athlete

Most professional athletes are a nervous bunch of guys because they are insecure about their future. Hockey players know, although they may not admit it at first, that their life as hockey players is brief. At best, they may last fifteen years, that is if they are lucky enough not to be sidelined with broken backs, eye injuries, broken hips or broken something or another.

What does a hockey player do after his

playing days are over? Does he start looking for a job after age thirty or thirty-five? He has to, naturally. Starting a second career at that age is difficult, particularly when he hasn't done anything in his life but play hockey. Meanwhile, his school friends have worked at their trades or professions. To an athlete, the one disturbing thought is being an ex-athlete some day.

I have had my share of sleepless nights, worrying about my future. Even as a coach I worry. My life has been all hockey with nothing to fall back on but the ability to take a bunch of boys and mold them into a team. I have been fortunate enough to have made the switch from a player to a coach, and lucky enough to be able to work with boys who wanted to win games and championships.

I was seventeen when the New York Rangers scouts spotted me. One morning a well-dressed gentleman knocked on our door in Winnipeg with the hopes of convincing Dad that I should sign up with the Rangers. Selling Dad on the prospects of a professional hockey career for his son was like telling him that his work ethics had no meaning.

I thought Dad would never sign my contract without a fight. I was even afraid that he might embarrass the scout by calling hockey players bums. Well, I should have had more confidence in his judgment, because he was interested in my future. The scout could not convince him that the professional hockey player was better treated and paid more than the previous generation of hockey players. Dad kept asking:

"What's the future in hockey?"

"They are making more money," the scout tried to convince Dad. "The training camps are like hotels, and during the summer the boys have lots of time to look for another job."

The scout was talking like a salesman, and he figured Dad would be delighted to get rid of his son. Well, Dad let the man talk and after he had finished talking, Dad turned to him and said:

"You know what Clancey and Jackson and Richard did after the hockey season was over? They had to find jobs or starve to death. Even your Patrick boys were paid little."

In those days, the general impression was that it was nice to be in professional hockey for a few years, but could you find a job? The people had pity for these hockey players who worked so hard to play the game and didn't make any money. There was nothing glamorous about being in the big leagues in those days, and Dad let the scout know exactly how he felt.

"But those days are gone," the scout said.

"Freddie is a good student and I want him

to have a good education so he can find a good job."

"College!" The scout grasped the bargaining point. "Oh, we'll take care of that."

"You'll send my Freddie to college?" Dad asked repeatedly to get a definite commitment.

After repeated assurances of a college education for me to be paid by the Rangers organization, Dad signed my contract. I was to play for the New York Rovers of the Eastern United States Amateur Hockey League.

Later, Lester Patrick (one of the Patrick boys, as Dad called him), manager of the New York Rangers in the NHL and head of the N.Y. Rovers, told the press:

"Fred is a crackerjack of a student. In fact, we're going to go out of our way to see that he gets the best schooling possible."

Dad had insisted on a medical school for me, and promises were made by the Rangers organization to take care of my higher education.

But as it turned out, the immigrant Russian was outfoxed by a lot of slick talk. Since the verbal promise was not a part of the written contract, I never did go to medical school. Hockey, therefore, became a profession with its sleepless nights and worries about the future rather than my ticket to a higher education.

At the time, however, I didn't worry too much about my life. I was glad to be with the

Rangers organization which treated me just like the other players. At the ripe age of twenty-two, manager-coach Frank Boucher sent me packing to the St. Paul Saints of the United States Hockey League. Boucher told the press:

"Our move in no way reflects dissatisfaction with the Winnipeg rear-guard's work. He just wasn't getting enough work with the National League club."

Boucher's statement was accurate enough. It's true I wasn't getting enough ice-time. A rookie always suffers from an inferiority complex because his career is at the mercy of his coach. While on the bench, no rookie gets the experience of working out with the other members of his team and has a hard time getting over the shock of playing against stronger teams.

In a way I was glad that he had decided to send me to St. Paul. At least I would get more ice-time, which I did. But playing for St. Paul wasn't the same as playing for the Rangers. Wearing the Rangers uniform was a matter of pride, and now my pride was hurt. There was nothing I could do but play for St. Paul and improve my game. But I always wondered whether the Rangers organization would want me back. I am sure baseball and football players feel the same way when they are sent to the farm clubs.

Later that year after I was recalled by the

Rangers from St. Paul, I was considered a leading contender for the Calder Trophy, which is given to the NHL's leading rookie each year.

Not all players are equally talented, and a coach has no right to demand more than the player can produce. A few players, however, always perform better from the start because they have an instinct to anticipate plays. They remove the element of surprise by superior judgment. Of course, such players are few.

But then there are others who need the coach's special sixth sense to bring out their talents. One of the ways to do this is by pairing them with better players during an actual game. In most cases, the mediocre players will take on the confidence of their teammates. The adrenalin will start running through their systems and bring out their best efforts.

Generally, coaches will give less ice-time to mediocre players and will overwork the superstars on the team. So by the time playoffs come around, the coach is left with his superstars hurting and aching all over. He also has a bunch of mediocre players who have remained so because he didn't give them enough ice-time during the season. So what does a coach have on his hands? A team with exhausted superstars and less confident mediocre players who have no desire to win.

Lester Patrick put Allan Stanley and me on

the same defense line, and somehow we fit together like two peas in a pod. We complemented each other so well that our lack of experience didn't show.

In fact, I scored my first goal in professional hockey as a defenseman for the Rangers when we played Detroit Red Wings in Detroit. I was twenty-two years old at the time, and Detroit had thrown a formidable line of Ted Lindsay, Sid Abel and Pete Horeck against us. I think Gordie Howe was benched with a knee injury. Ted Lindsay's performance impressed me that night. Of all the big leaguers I have played against, Maurice Richard of the Canadians and Lindsay of the Wings were the foxiest forwards I have faced.

As my performance improved, the Rangers coach Patrick, who was called the silver fox, paid me a compliment when he said:

"Shero is the most underrated player of the Rangers. If he keeps improving as he has done this season (1949-50), Shero won't have a peer among the league's defensemen."

I like being the best, but compliment or not, Patrick traded me to the Cleveland Barons in 1951. Suddenly my performance had dropped, and the Rangers organization couldn't figure out what my problem was, so the best thing for them to do was to trade me.

After acquiring me from the Rangers organization, the Barons organization sent me to

Seattle for most of the 1952–53 season. Manager Jim Hendy of the Barons had spotted my problem. He said it was my poor eyesight and persuaded me to wear glasses when I came back in mid-season. The next season Hendy bought me a pair of contact lenses.

These lenses were not the most comfortable things to wear, but I didn't have to hesitate to move in when I saw I had a break. When I wore glasses, I was not quite anxious to get tangled or take a chance at close range. But with the contacts, I was ready to hussle. As a result, my game improved once again and during my best season I scored 17 goals. Most of the goals came from near the net.

Had it not been for those two little plastic disks, I would have been out of the game a long time ago, and possibly selling groceries somewhere.

A professional athlete's life is not easy. The pressures of trying to put out 100 percent every time could turn an average person old before his time. Certainly, it isn't the most secure job in the world. But it can be rewarding, if the coach is astute enough to use his players effectively.

But what happens when the knees buckle and the reflexes slow down? Does he tend bar and drown his sorrow or become a stockbroker?

chapter 5

Violence in Hockey

My first experience on defense came at the N.Y. Rangers training camp in Winnipeg in 1943. Frank Boucher, the playing-coach of the Rangers asked me to try out on defense my very first day because he was short of defensemen. It seemed that every time I scrimmaged against Boucher, I stopped him easily. Somehow, he always got the puck tangled up in my feet. This seemed to impress him and he signed me to a contract with the New York Rovers of the E.H.L. for the grand sum of $1,000 for the year.

I believe it was at Christmastime that New York, with an abundance of young hockey players, decided to form another team in the same league, called the Brooklyn Crescents. They asked me to join that team. I formed a line with Fernie Flaman and Gopher Ashworth and we were called the Pony Line. All this time, I performed as a forward. I did not start playing defense regularly until 1945–46 under coach Fred Metcalfe of the New York Rangers.

It was December 1948 and I was playing for the St. Paul Saints of the United States Hockey League. Since I was still under contract to the New York Rangers organization, I could be recalled anytime the Rangers needed me. I was hoping—more like praying—that I would be recalled to wear the Rangers uniform, and my prayers were answered early one morning. It was 2:30 A.M. when the phone rang: Muzz Patrick of the Rangers was calling me from Chicago. He was desperate. They recalled me with two games left in the regular St. Paul season which was against the rules and subject to a $10,000 fine. This really impressed me.

"Pick up your equipment and join the Rangers in Chicago tomorrow for a game with the Black Hawks," Patrick blurted and hung up.

I couldn't make the early train to Chicago, because my equipment was still tucked away at the arena in Minneapolis. I picked up my equipment later that morning, flew to Chicago, managed to poke some food down my throat, then tried to grab a few hours of sleep before game time.

When I reported for the game, Frank Boucher took me aside and said, "Fred, I think with your boxing talent, you'll be a good defenseman for us."

"What's boxing got to do with defense?"

"You're going to hustle Chicago with muscle," he said calmly.

"Why me? You've bigger fellows on the team."

"Big yes, but they can't fight. You're a boxer and our team needs more punch," said Boucher in a tone that meant the conversation had come to an end.

"Well, I'll try."

One didn't disagree with a coach in those days. Besides, this was my chance to get back with the Rangers and I wasn't about to allow a change in style to dampen my enthusiasm.

I was glad to be back with the Rangers, but this sudden turn of events was quite unexpected and it bothered me. Since I didn't want to disappoint Boucher, I hit Chicago that night.

But there was more to the game than just hitting—there was a new system. The Rangers under Fred Metcalfe's influence decided to try a new tactic never before used in the N.H.L. We tried it successfully and beat Chicago easily 4-1. The system is a 2-2-1 system of forechecking. We call the first two men half-backs, the second two men full-backs, and the third a stopper. In other words, we really had only one defenseman in the other team's zone. It bewildered Chicago.

The press joyfully reported that I was "the thundering thumper of the blue line" and talked openly about my boxing background. Perhaps the idea of a boxer playing professional hockey had an unusual appeal that the press could not resist. I was flattered, no doubt.

Although I took up boxing when I was ten years old, I never did like hurting people. I began boxing quite by accident. One of my brothers had become interested in boxing. I imagine it was Dad's influence. Dad was fascinated with boxing primarily because it was the only sport that had gained international recognition. He figured that anyone who was lucky enough to make it to the top had a fortune waiting for him. My brother thought he would give Dad's dream a whirl.

While his enthusiasm for boxing waned after a week, my interest grew. I kept trekking back to the arena a few nights a week when there was no hockey. The arena was about seven miles away, so I had to walk fourteen miles all alone in the bitter cold. Sometimes, I would try a shortcut that trimmed the distance down to a six-mile roundtrip, but this shortcut had its dangers. It took me through the dark and deserted railroad yards, across the fields and through back alleys. There was always the danger of being mauled by wolves and wild dogs or being chased by drunks and thieves. Once, a pack of wolves trailed me to the edge of town, the hair on their backs bristling in the cold. But they never came close enough to do any harm.

At the arena, two ex-boxers felt that I showed promise as a boxer and decided to work with me. As a lad of ten I was looking for guidance and thought myself fortunate to be trained by not one but two ex-boxers. Seaman Smart was an Englishman with an unshakable belief in classical boxing, stand-up style. Bobby Siegal, an American ex-boxer who had drifted into the Winnipeg area, knew only one style.

"Bob and weave, hit your opponent, one, two," he kept repeating in his gravel voice. American boxers are known for their rough-house technique, the street brawler style of going after your opponent as if he were your mortal enemy. I picked up both styles and managed to mix them up with convincing authority against my opponents. I could handle myself against anybody. Yet, in spite of this latent courage to face any opponent, I was always afraid before every fight. I would be worried even if I had to fight my brother. But that fear would disappear as soon as I touched gloves. Then I was ready to go.

In 1940 I was fifteen years old and the holder of the bantamweight and flyweight championships of Manitoba. Later, in the Canadian Navy, I boxed a lot. I also won the Canadian Navy's middleweight championship. After I was discharged from the navy, just before the Second World War ended, my two trainers were after me to turn professional. But I turned down all offers because I still had a contract with the New York Rangers. Besides, I loved hockey more than boxing.

I have never enjoyed hurting people except in self-defense; even then, I am liable to turn the other cheek. I am hardly a saint, but I know the power I have in my fists. They could be very damaging if I ever have to use them against someone. In fact, I almost killed an opponent once and that experience turned me off; and in a way, made the decision for me to go into hockey instead of professional boxing.

I was still in the Canadian Navy and flying all over the country to box visiting champions from the British and American armed services. Once I was scheduled to box an Australian champion. The bout was held in the small town of Paulson, Manitoba. It was a navy town and wasn't even on the map.

I was the headliner and billed as the star of the Canadian Navy. About 3,000 servicemen had gathered at the base. Betting was furious;

The NHL's only coaching triumvirate: Shero, Mike Nykoluk and Barry Ashbee at practice with, from left: Reggie Leach, Bobby Clarke, Ted Harris, Ed Van Impe and Bill Barber. Shero tries to make the grueling practice sessions enjoyable for his players by conducting unusual drills, games, etc. Not a single Flyer has missed a practice in over two years, a most revealing statistic.

(*Opposite*) Philadelphia Inquirer columnist Bill Lyon quotes Billy Harris of Islanders: ". . . People keep talking about (the Flyers) intimidating you. That's a lot of bleep. That's not what beats you. It's the way they play, the way they check, the way they always seem to be where they're supposed to be . . . It's like sleeping with a pillow on top of your face . . ." Ed Van Impe and Jim Watson demonstrate defense technique in front of Flyer goalie Wayne Stephenson. Van Impe muscles Islander wing Clark Gillies, while Watson blocks off Ralph Stewart. (*Below*) The Master lectures. Shero holds court with Jim Watson, Ross Lonsberry, Andre Dupont, Bill Barber, Reg Leach, Bobby Clarke, Gary Dornhoefer and Bernie Parent during a pre-season practice session.

With Watson patrolling the blue line, Van Impe poke-checks the puck away from J. P. Parise.

"It's not nice to antagonize Flyers' fans." Islander goalie Glenn "Chico" Resch bears brunt of Spectrum jeers after his comments about Flyers in general and their defense in particular. Flyers shut out Resch and Islanders 4-0 in first playoff game.

Shero with two of the voices of national hockey telecasts, Tim Ryan and Ted Lindsey. Ryan has been critical of the Flyers' rough-house style, and his comment last year about Bobby Clarke's "dirty" style of play brought howls of outrage from Flyer fans. Lindsey, himself a brilliant player for the Detroit Redwings during the 50's and 60's, likes the Flyers style of play. Perhaps his affection for the Flyers stems from his own brawling technique during his playing days. He still holds the NHL record for career penalty minutes with over 1800 . . . a record Dave Schultz seems destined to eclipse.

Shero with Dave Schultz and Bob Kelly. Player to Schultz' right is Rick Foley, one of the few disciplinary problems Shero has ever had. Foley was a big, tough, mean defenseman obtained from Chicago in a trade that sent popular Flyer Andre Lacroix to the Blackhawks. Foley was eventually let go by the Flyers because of his refusal to reduce to the playing weight Shero wanted. When he wouldn't cooperate, he was released, even though he was skilled offensively. As always with Shero, team play takes precedence over individual play.

The 1972 amateur draft brought these five young hopefuls to Philadelphia. When the picture was taken, no one could know that the three kids in the center, Tom Bladon, Jim Watson and Bill Barber would become key players in the Flyers' Stanley Cup conquest. Barber and Watson have already been selected NHL All Stars, and Bladon set a scoring record for Flyer defensemen. The two players on the end are Darryl Fudorak, left, and Alan MacAdam, far right. MacAdam was traded to the California Golden Seals in the deal that brought Reggie Leach to the Flyers. Fudorak never made it in the NHL.

A study in intensity behind the bench, Shero makes a point with a player.

(*Above*) These shots usually won't hurt you. Islanders' Jude Drouin fires at Shephenson from outside blue line. (*Opposite*) These shots will hurt you! Dennis Potvin scores a critical goal in third period of second playoff game. Islanders scored twice in 14 seconds to send game into sudden-death. Flyers won at 2:56 of overtime on goal by the incomparable Bobby Clarke.

An early season practice session during Shero's second year. Only two players are still with team; Bill Clement (third from left) and Dave Schultz (far right). Those departed or still in the minors include Wayne

lman, Rick Foley, Simonet Nolet, Rene Drolet and Bob Currier. If you k closely, you see Bernie Parent in goal behind the group during his st stint with the Flyers.

(*Above*) Spectrum has become sign capital of the league. Flyer's fans regularly festoon the rink with the most orginal banners to be found anywhere. Philadelphia even features nationally-known "Sign-Man", Dave Leonardi, a New Jersey school teacher who regularly brings over 100 signs to every home game. Banners are especially prominent during nationally-televised games. (*Below*) Over 17,000 fanatics jam the Spectrum for every Flyers game. Just before opening face-off of second semi-final playoff game at Spectrum.

The man who brought the Cup to Philadelphia . . . and another championship ring to his finger.

the Australian's size and age made me an eight-to-one underdog. I was only eighteen at the time, while my opponent was twenty-five and boasted openly about his experience. He had fought in London and Sidney, demolished opponents in Bombay and Hong Kong.

I figured this was going to be one of those regular bouts where two fellows step into the ring, box around a few rounds and one is declared a winner. I arrived the night before the bout and found myself bunking with the burly Australian. The fellows in the bunkhouse asked me if I had seen my opponent, when the Australian swaggered into the sprawling shelter with a chip on his shoulder. I later realized it was more like a log that he was carrying: he was looking for trouble. I tried to be friendly, so I extended my hand. But he only glared at me and gnashed his teeth as if I were his late night snack and he was about to reduce me to pieces.

He looked down his nose at me and blurted in an Australian accent:

"I'm going to kill ya, ya Canuck."

Between ill-conceived profanities and a lot of body English, he made it clear to me that he hated Canadians, that we were lousy fighters, that we strutted around in stiff uniforms like the British and lived in igloos like women.

I have met many boxers and hockey players as an athlete, but never again have I been put through an experience that made me so mad. I didn't know whether I should punch him right there, which I could have done with ease, or try to figure this guy out.

I suddenly realized that this wasn't going to be just another bout between two servicemen, but a bout of gladiators with a lot of blood spilt. I made up my mind then that it wasn't going to be mine.

He kept egging me on in the mess hall the next morning and followed me around like the plague. He was trying to make me mad and knew that he was getting the upper hand. The bout was scheduled for six rounds but it never went the full distance. The referee stopped the bout in the fourth round because my opponent was in no condition to continue. I knocked him down six or seven times and his face looked like the inside of a tomato. I was told that it took thirty or forty stitches to patch up his face.

Luckily for him, they stopped the bout, otherwise I would have killed the guy. The next day he came over to me and tried to be friendly. His attitude toward me had changed, and he was suddenly in a mood to explain to me his method of psyching himself. He confessed that taunting his opponents had always worked beautifully in his favor, but after this bout he was going to have to find some other way to build up courage.

It's ironic that the Rangers wanted me back

with the team to punch the opposition. I had turned down boxing offers because I was tired of getting into that ring and knocking other people's brains out.

Most hockey coaches don't realize that a player has difficulty mixing boxing with hockey. The two sports require different sets of muscles. When I trained for boxing, I skipped rope, shadow boxed and did road work which involved a twelve-mile run. In hockey, a player does a lot of gliding because his legs have to do a lot of smooth work. Boxers develop the upper part of their bodies, while in hockey the concentration is on the lower part of the body.

Boucher was right when he said that the bigger guys on the team couldn't fight. Obviously their training hadn't included a course in boxing. But it wasn't boxing that the Rangers were interested in: it was violence.

Hockey statistics show that the winning team usually has more penalties to its credit. In 1947, for instance, the Toronto Maple Leafs were the most penalized club in the league. Yet, they won the regular season race and the Stanley Cup Championship. Lester Patrick was fond of pointing out that fact; he thought that if he could get me to intimidate the opposition and keep them off balance, the Rangers would manage to score more goals. When Boucher was coaching the team, the Rangers recorded 151 minutes of penalties in the first twenty-three games. Under Patrick's aggressive coaching, the penalties jumped and we were hit for 67 minutes in eight games.

Patrick summed up his thoughts on aggression when he gave us a short pep talk on December 21, 1949:

"Don't take any nonsense from anybody. Anything you get you give back double. I want an aggressive man on my team. When the puck is out in the corner against the boards, I want my player to be the one to come out with the puck."

This, to me, was good hockey. Being aggressive is part of the game. Earlier, he had remarked that the Rangers lacked punch. "This is not a class team," he observed. But the team of Frank Boucher and Lester Patrick turned us around. We began out-hustling the opposition.

I was teamed with Allan Stanley, and Patrick began rotating Bill Moe, Wally Stanowski and Frank Eddolls as his other defensemen. Moe, one of the few American players in the National League, enjoyed roughhouse hockey. He was quite popular in New York. The fans would go wild whenever he checked an opponent. He did it with a football-style block which usually stopped the opposition, but also took Moe out of the play.

My dislike of violence became known to Boucher. I cut down on unnecessary fighting with opposing players, and my penalty statistics weren't too impressive. Soon, word got around that Boucher was making a special trip to New Haven, Connecticut, to look over the New York Rovers because he was unhappy with Moe and me. I played 138 games for the Rangers from 1947 to 1950. Finally, I was farmed to Cincinnati and, still later, I was sold to the Cleveland Barons in 1951.

I have never objected to legal body blows in hockey, but I am opposed to violence on the ice. Of course, I have participated in my share of fighting, but I have never enjoyed punching a hockey player in the mouth or any other part of his anatomy. Coaches are notorious for making unreasonable demands on their hockey players. No coach has the right to tell his players to fight the opposition. Body checks? Yes. Fights and violence? No.

My refusal to continue fighting for the Rangers was the major reason why they didn't want me. In those days, the Rangers organization wanted aggressive players who could do damage. Even when I was with the New York Rovers in New York, I was asked to fight. It makes me wonder now whether I was drafted by the Rangers organization because of my hockey talents or my ability to flatten an opponent with a punch.

Ed MacCawley, the New York Rangers goalie in 1943-44, received a concussion in Detroit in 1944. While he was recuperating, he was asked to help coach the Brooklyn Crescents of the E.H.L., the team I was playing with at the time.

He said bluntly: "Fred, if you don't hit everything that moves tonight, I'm shipping you home."

The words still ring in my ears. My survival in the world of hockey was at stake. The thought of being dismissed by the farm club was unbearable. I couldn't even think of crawling back to Winnipeg to tell Dad that my professional hockey career was over before it had even begun. At eighteen, I had already begun to feel the pressures of professional hockey.

So when the puck dropped on the red line that evening, I began a systematic rampage to flatten the opposition. I didn't even know who we were playing. But it didn't matter. I hit everything that moved in the rink, including the goalie. The coach's threat had transformed me from a 150-pound hockey player into a terror on ice, and the opposition knew it.

The fear of being shipped home had made me mad. I hated the coach more than I hated the opposition for putting fear in me. Since I couldn't hit the coach, I came down hard on the opposition. I was ready to fight even King Kong that night. My bone-crunching checks and blows intimidated the fellows, who were about my age, and I didn't even know them. They turned and ran and lost.

Of late, much has been made of violence in hockey. Critics of the game have exaggerated somewhat the nature of violence. Perhaps they have been swayed by the need for good copy. During this time, our news media have proven that violence in any form makes good copy. In the Viet Nam era, the public was fed large doses of violence on television, in newspapers and in magazines. But that's war, critics say; war is never clean. Well, I agree. War is hell, but it also has its news value.

But you cannot equate the violence of war with the aggressiveness of hockey players on the ice. Hockey is hardly a war.

Everybody admits that hockey is a very aggressive sport, and some body checks look violent. Isolating a 30-second skirmish in a slow-motion replay for the benefit of TV viewers has its morbid entertainment value. Such programming emphasizes the wrong things in hockey. Why don't the media show the stick handling of Bobby Orr, Bobby Hull, Frank Mahovlich, Stan Mikita or Flyer Rick MacLeish, as often as the fights?

I admit that the media never try to play favorites and will hunt violence in sports whenever it occurs. But when a reporter equates the idea of violence with the aggressive nature of hockey and comes up with a criticism of the game, he is doing a disservice.

I am really surprised, however, that there is not more violence in hockey, since it is the only game in which players come armed with sticks in their hands and sharp blades on their feet. These are really dangerous weapons if used improperly, and the players are quite capable of mutilating an opponent's face or breaking his back. One almost broke mine. But the credit for keeping the injuries down goes to the players and to the referees.

At times, a rookie referee can make players mad with a wrong decision. The players are on the ice to win; they have enough problems with the opposition without having to fight the referee's decisions, particularly when he is wrong.

I was coaching the St. Paul Saints in 1962. On a Sunday in January, we were playing the Minneapolis Millers, our arch rivals. Referee George Karn made our goalie Jacques Marcotte mad with a delayed penalty call on the Saints' Paul Mesnick in the second period.

Karn said that Marcotte hit him with a stick and then started a brawl by the penalty box. Marcotte explained, "We're playing for first place and they put these rookie officials in the game. I tell him I don't like the penalty and he tells me to get back in my cage."

President Lou Kaplan of the Saints blamed Commissioner Frank Gallagher. According to

Kaplan, the commissioner shouldn't have put Karn in the game after the skirmish he and Marcotte had had the previous Thursday night in the all-star game in St. Paul.

"I don't excuse Marcotte's behavior," Kaplan added, "but with smarter scheduling the situation might have been avoided."

The St. Paul hockey club was fined $500 the heaviest penalty ever given one hockey team in the fifteen-year history of the International Hockey League. Four key players, besides Marcotte, were suspended. Marcotte was out for the season, while the others were suspended for two or three days.

The commissioner's decision stunned the St. Paul club. The players became furious when the Millers' coach said, "I'm convinced we've got superior personnel to St. Paul's and only Jacques Marcotte in the nets keeps the Saints in the IHL race."

Mickey Keating, our defenseman, countered: "He'll find out that no one man is bigger than a team effort. Sure Marcotte is superb, but his loss only got us aroused that much more. We defensemen realize that we've got to skate all-out and give full protection to Al Davis or whoever is in the nets. Yackel will find out that this is a solid team and that we can win with Uncle Fud in the pads."

When we met Minneapolis the following Friday, St. Paul won 8–1. In my three years with the Saints, I had never seen them skate more brilliantly, although they had every reason to collapse under suspensions and injuries.

I would hate to be on a team that took on the Flyers if Bernie Parent were suspended for the season. No club has a better team spirit than the Flyers—these boys would rally around and demolish the opposition.

During a game, hockey players are tense. Their nerves are on edge, ready to pop. A wrong decision by the officials would be just as disturbing to them as a hard body check. Unlike football and baseball, which are comparatively slow games, hockey is played at a feverish pitch. The players are moving at speeds of twenty-five to thirty miles an hour; when two bodies collide, they feel the impact.

Hockey players, therefore, have to be more mature than football or baseball players. They can't allow the other team's offensive tactics to goad them into making too many mistakes.

A hockey team has forwards, defensemen and a goalie. It does not have special offensive and defensive squads. Everyone plays offensively or defensively. The team that takes the offensive has a better chance of winning than a defensive team. But the offensive nature of the game should not be confused with violence.

Offensive hockey requires body checks, and a good legal body check that dumps the opposition gives the team an advantage of two on one or three on two. What may appear to be threats of violence to the fans and critics are nothing more than harassment tactics.

For instance, a defenseman and a goalie may slash or jab the opposition's forward who is parked right in front of the net. They want him out of there because he is waiting to deflect the puck coming his way from his wings or a rebound from the boards.

Sometimes the harassment becomes aggressive and may even frighten the forward, who doesn't want constant jabs in the ribs or sticks in his face. He will, therefore, move to a safer spot. When he does move away from his advantageous position, he usually misses the chance to deflect the puck in the net.

A high scorer like Phil Esposito of the Boston Bruins has scored many goals from such close quarters because of his dogged determination to stay in front of the opposition's net in spite of cross checks and slashes and elbows in the face. Bobby Clarke also patrols the area in front of the net and will not give in to threats of violence.

One must realize that hockey is full of intimidations and often these attempts to terrorize do result in violence. If the opposition allows itself to be terrorized, for instance, it will lose the offensive edge and, finally, the game. Many a goal has been scored by dumping the star player and taking him out of the game. During my playing days, my teammates called me Ferocious Freddy. The other teams called me something else.

Some critics label the Flyers a violent team. Yet, these same critics will applaud if Clarke or MacLeish or Schultz is dealt a stiff body check. The Flyers are an aggressive team, no doubt, and they are going to stay aggressive. But aggression alone doesn't win games and a championship. It takes discipline, teamwork, conditioning and a "system."

chapter 6
Some Training Techniques

Among some parents there is a feeling that a professional athlete, like a ballet dancer, has to be reared from the cradle. Parents will make up their minds that their son is going to be a football or a hockey player, then they will shower him with equipment and send him to clinics until the boy is tired of the whole thing. Often parents come to me and say, "I want my son to be a hockey player, and I don't want him to play any other sport."

Well, these parents are foolish to think that way. A boy of five does not need the rigorous training of a hockey player to become a Gordie Howe, a Bobby Hull, a Phil Esposito or a Bobby Clarke. I am told that a ballet dancer has to start young so that a particular set of muscles can be trained and developed in a specific way. A ballet student can't go horseback riding, for instance, because a different set of muscles are used when riding a horse than those used for performing the various ballet moves.

Hockey, like most sports, doesn't have these restrictions or rigors. The firstborn, therefore, doesn't have to start hockey practice the day after he switches from diapers to toilet training.

Lynn and Muzz Patrick, two of the most outstanding hockey players to come out of Canada, never even started playing hockey till they were fourteen. Ivan Irwin was another late starter at the age of thirteen or fourteen. Although they didn't start as hockey players at an early age, they did participate in other sports like football, soccer and even baseball. The point is that they were all good athletes to begin with. They had the natural ability and coordination to play sports.

I had my best year in hockey when I turned sixteen or seventeen. At that age I boxed a lot, at least once a week. For that one bout, I would put in fifteen rounds of practice three times a week. This included three rounds of skipping rope, three rounds of shadow boxing, three rounds with the heavy bag, three more with the small bag and I topped it off with three rounds of sparring.

And after that heavy workout, I still had enough energy to put in two hours on the ice every morning. That was the time when I made the all-star hockey team, and I think it was the greatest year of my life. Then came the New York Rangers organization. Overnight I had become a pro, so my attitude toward training changed, and I began to ape the others on the pro team. These guys did nothing compared to my workouts, so I did nothing. Instead of doing fifteen rounds of boxing to keep in shape, I did three rounds of beer.

Conditioning is very important for a professional or even an amateur athlete. It is not necessary for a hockey player to play too many practice games during the season, but he has to keep in shape. Instead of playing hockey, he should get involved in other sports. Soccer will develop his legs, and he should get in a few games of tennis to develop his wind.

My advice to parents is to allow their children to play all types of sports. Let the kid just develop his natural coordination and understand what it is to compete with other kids his own age. He must know how to get along with his peer group and be able to share things with others on the team. I remember playing soccer from the time I could run fast enough to kick the ball away from the bigger boys who were in the second grade.

Soccer is a good game for hockey players. I played soccer and later picked up American-style football. In fact, all the boys who played hockey in winter spent their summers playing soccer and football. Soccer builds the legs and feet, puts strength in the lower part of the body and makes a hockey player a good puck handler with his feet.

Today's hockey players don't use their feet to manipulate the puck. I think the reason could be that they are playing little soccer now that they are professionals. This is one area where the Canadian players have regressed. The Russian and the European hockey players, however, are experts in this area of play.

In Russia, the training of an athlete has become a science. While visiting that country with a study group from the University of Loyola in June 1974, I had the opportunity to visit many facilities where boys and girls were in training to become future Olympic gold medallists in all areas of sports, including hockey.

All the kids in these facilities start out with gymnastic drills, and they seem to be in better physical condition than the Canadian and American boys and girls of the same age. Interestingly enough, the Russian coaches will not allow these youngsters to get on the ice and play hockey until they are twelve or thirteen years old. Their training methods are such that a young athlete who wants to become a hockey player must be proficient in every sport before that youngster is allowed to strap on hockey skates. These boys and girls play soccer and basketball, ride horses and swim, and the boys box.

The object of the Russian method seems to be a concentrated effort to give the youngster an all-round training, to give the child a feel for all sports. Such a system helps to develop the entire body and condition the mind.

But in Canada, what do hockey players do? They will concentrate only on their legs, but do nothing substantial for their upper bodies. Sure, they will lift weights to put more bulk on the arms and chest. But does that develop strength in the arms, shoulders, chest and back? Weight lifting may even make them sluggish and slow on the ice. As long as I have played hockey, nobody did anything for the upper part of the body with the exception of one person. Bill Ezinicki did push-ups before a game religiously; all the other guys on the team thought he was nuts.

Even today, hockey players take their strength for granted and feel embarrassed to do exercises in front of their teammates. When I first suggested to the Flyers that they should do certain exercises, they were reluctant. But their skepticism didn't last long. Now it is fun to watch them, because they are always competing with each other.

Like the Russians, we are constantly exercising. During the season, the boys perform certain drills which strengthen the body. We play tennis during our off days or we might even have swimming contests. The Russians play every sport during the course of the year, not confining themselves to hockey drills. The coaches in Russia encourage their players to go mountain climbing and skiing during the winter and play soccer during the summer.

I agree with the philosophy that every hockey player must be a master at all sports, because hockey combines all sports. When I was in the big leagues, the hockey players were generally proficient in soccer, football, baseball, skiing, swimming, basketball and even horseback riding. These boys were picked from the best athletes in their area.

But today that is not the case. They get a sixteen-year-old who knows how to skate and is pretty fair at handling the puck and the coach will immediately tell him that he can't play any other sport. These boys, therefore, don't know how to body check because they have never played football—which involves a lot of body contact. They may have played touch football which has little body contact.

Since hockey is a game of body contact, these boys like to hit, but they don't know how. They are bigger and stronger than the boys from my generation, but they cannot body check without losing their balance or hurting themselves.

During my playing days, coaches treated their players as if they were mindless boobs to be used as battering rams to bowl over the opposition. I remember times when we would cross over to the other side of the street if we saw our coach coming down the sidewalk. The coaches had made the players feel so inferior that we were afraid even to say "good evening" to them. Most coaches gave the impression that they were godlike, and the attitude at that time was not to question the coach even if what he said didn't make sense.

If a player was bold enough to suggest an idea, he was immediately put in his place. When I became a coach years ago, I put aside the traditional thinking of building a gulf between a coach and his players. I wanted to test my players and I wanted them to test me. I don't ever want my players to be afraid of me. If they find that I am doing something that they don't think is good for the team, I want them to come to me and tell me without having to beat around the bush.

I have come to realize that players want to know why I am asking them to do certain drills and execute specific plays, and I like that approach. The more questions they ask, the more they learn. The participation of players is necessary if a coach is going to be successful with new techniques and systems. The players must be allowed freedom to express their ideas. Once a coach allows his players to think for themselves, he is creating better athletes. When a player knows that his ideas are welcome, he feels that he is contributing more to improve the game and his team's performance than just scoring goals or assists or hitting people. On my team, everybody contributes his physical and mental abilities.

This concept of being the total athlete is very much a part of the game. In hockey, more than in any other professional sport, mental ability is equally as important as physical strength. There are no huddles in hockey and nobody can run out of bounds to stop the play. Nobody can call time out and run to the sidelines for instructions from the coach.

In hockey, the player is forced to make split-second decisions. I firmly believe that a well-educated hockey player can become a superb hockey player with proper training and preseason conditioning by a coach who has a system. It could be any system, as long as it is one that enables players to work together and coordinate their plays.

During the 1940s, Frank Boucher, who coached the New York Rangers, made a statement that exemplifies the lack of depth most coaches have brought to the game. He said:

"There's no use trying to plan our game from the sidelines. A hockey player is like a woman. He can change his mind as often as he likes. He can go anywhere on the ice that he thinks offers him a scoring chance. All I can do is hope he is right—and that he gets there fast."

This thinking may have been good for Boucher, because in those days the game was still in its infancy. Although coaches are not expected to think along these lines today, one has only to watch many of the teams on the ice to wonder if Boucher's ghost is still lurking behind the benches. While the Russians and the Europeans have made a science of the game, we continue to stumble along blindly with primitive ideas that should have been discarded a long time ago.

chapter 7

Thoughts on Coaching

The hockey season of 1957–58 brought me to the small town of Shawinigan, about ninety miles north of Montreal. My back injury, suffered almost eight years before, had made the decision for me. With a bum back, a hockey player has nowhere to go in the sport, except to become a coach if a club will give him a chance.

I received the injury when I was with the Cleveland Barons. We were in Pittsburgh for the first game of the season in 1951. Leo Boivin put his stick across my back as I whirled around. I felt the jolt but dismissed it, hoping the pain would eventually go away after a shower and a night's rest.

But my back twisted again in the second game in Providence. I couldn't even bend over to lace my skates. Dr. F. J. Mackley, the team physician for the Barons, announced that I also had two cracked ribs.

"Muscle spasms in the region of the spine are delaying Fred's complete recovery," he told the coach and manager. He was right. Although my ribs were healed, the recurring back pains kept me on the sidelines for the rest of the season. Talk began to circulate that my career was in jeopardy. But I managed to bounce back and I played for the Barons for four more years before signing with the Winnipeg Warriors, a new entry in the Western Hockey League in 1955. Coach Alfie Pike had no misgivings about my back injury, and I was proud to be named captain of the team.

But once again I injured my back while playing against the Calgary Stampeders in the last game of the series. We were in Vancouver, British Columbia, at the time. My recovery was important to the team and no less important to me. But when I overheard the doctors talking about operating on my back, I got into my street clothes, strapped my back tight and quietly dropped out of the hospital window to disappear into the night.

I managed to reach a hotel and went to sleep. I am glad that I decided to leave the hospital early that night. If I had waited a little longer, the fast-acting sleeping pills would have left me stranded on a sidewalk or a park bench.

My caper convinced the doctors and the team's management that I was not about to let anybody open up my back, regardless of the consequences. I stayed with the Warriors for two seasons, then decided that it was time for me to look for another career. I was thirty-one.

I had ventured into business before, thinking of just such an eventuality when I might have to give up the game. I had tried the contracting business and later operated a vending machine enterprise, but business was not for me. Hockey and sports had been my life, so I turned to coaching.

Fortunately for me, the Shawinigan Falls Cataracts of the Quebec Hockey League were looking for a player-coach. I took over from Roger Leger, who took over as coach for the Montreal Royals in the QHL. The Shawinigan team was made up of castoffs from the Montreal organization. The second string players were sent to the Montreal Royals, while the worst players were shunted to my team. I got the job because no coach wanted to be associated with a team that was going nowhere.

Instead of flashing my credentials and barking orders to the players, I took a softer approach. The barrier that usually arises between a new coach and players who are down on their luck was removed by using reverse psychology. I did not have to tell them that they were a bad team and had to improve. They already knew that. To threaten them was childish because they didn't care a damn.

So during our first meeting, I told them that I was quite new at coaching and needed their help. I made the team realize that this coach was not some superior being who was going to boss them around with pep talks and chest-thumping ultimatums. A rapport was immediately established. We were going to trade off our talents and exchange our knowledge of the game.

I selected Jerry Desaulniers as the captain of the team. He was in the same class as Bobby Clarke—not as a hockey player but as a leader. The players looked up to him. We decided that we had to do something, otherwise we were going to stay in the cellar for quite some time.

The result was astonishing: Shawinigan finished in second place in the playoffs. We had no business winning the games and placing so high in the standings, because we just didn't have the caliber of players to make a comeback in one year. Eventually, six of the players made it to the big leagues.

Take the Flyers, for instance. We had no reason, if reason is to be culled from statistics and scouting reports, to win the 1974 Stanley Cup Championship. There were other teams in the NHL with very superior personnel. Some of the players are even considered by pundits today as the best in hockey history. But the Flyers won the championship. The explanation goes beyond statistics and averages. There is no mathematical formula that can explain courage and confidence, and I doubt one will be forthcoming. The variables of the human experience, upbringing, training and instinct vary from player to player.

But unlike parents, a coach's stay with a team is not quite permanent. Wise parents have the opportunity to become wiser as they learn the art and science of parenthood. Fortunately for them, time is on their side. Often a second and third chance is given to them to try out their modified ideas of raising a son or a daughter.

But the coach of a professional team does not have time on his side. Above all, he suffers from a handicap that does not afflict parents. By the time a coach becomes wise enough to realize his mistakes and devise new methods to correct them, he is out on the street looking for a job. He is racing constantly against time, trying desperately to improve himself and his team. The daily span of twenty-four hours is insufficient time for the thinking, planning and worrying that must be done. Successful coaches, therefore, have to do all their thinking and planning long before they reach the major leagues, just like the lad who works behind the counter of his father's store or workshop. The lad picks up the business by osmosis.

Some observers may claim that fate had endowed me with early maturity, or a sense of purpose and judgment that is often denied a teenager. Fortunately for me, whatever precocity I possessed as a boy managed to reach fruition without denying me the pleasures of childhood. I suspect my father had a lot to do with it, keeping me tethered to a routine of work and play. I would have gladly reversed the proportions of these aspects of my early life had it been possible for me to influence him. If I had, the balance would have been destroyed.

My coaching career began quite early. To put it in perspective, my apprenticeship began during my teens, long before I reached the New York Rangers. While playing for the junior teams, my summers were free to explore the world. Somehow my world contained more than its share of social dropouts. In the summer of

1941, I noticed that the depression had become history, but its traces still lingered on in our neighborhood.

The summers brought out wandering gangs of boys venting frustrations, rather than channeling their energies in a purposeful way. They were drifting from one mischief to another and they needed some guidance and leadership.

So at the age of sixteen, I put together a baseball team. I became the manager, the coach, the big brother. We traveled all over town as a team. For some of the boys, this was the first experience of being part of a group that worked together, each one sacrificing for the team, learning to live with each other. I continued this practice during the summers even after I joined the pro ranks. My professional job as a major leaguer enabled me to spend more money on the team. We bought uniforms and extended our experience by visiting other neighboring towns.

My enthusiasm in helping the boys led me to develop a boxing team and a baseball team. I feel that a coach is like a professional manager in business: if he is disciplined and has developed a system, he has the capabilities to coach a team in any sport. If the premise holds good, then a college hockey coach should be able to make it coaching a professional team. The theory is credible but human nature destroys it.

I was one of the few who applauded the Detroit Red Wings organization's audacity when they brought in an accomplished college coach. Ned Harkness had been quite a successful coach at Cornell, and he was no stranger to hockey. But he was a stranger to professional hockey. His college education alienated him from most professional hockey players, many of whom were hostile to educated people. Since a majority of the players did not have a college education, Ned became a target of ridicule. It seems that the players made no attempt to understand him. He was having difficulty getting through to them.

Players began to harbor doubts about his ability to handle a professional team. Since conditions did not improve, the Detroit management felt pressured to remove him. It was partly Ned's fault. He kept referring to his Cornell days more frequently than the Wings wanted to hear about them. Perhaps if I were a Red Wing, I, too, would have disliked his constant references to Cornell days. However, I feel management should have stood behind him. On the other hand, there is little that management can do when there is a battle of two forces, with both coach and players feeling superior to each other and nobody willing to give in.

The switch from college to pro ranks may be glamorous for a player. But for a coach, it is quite different. If he hasn't come through the pro ranks, the players will turn on him. The players often feel they are part of a clique, an elite group, a secret society to which nobody from another area of the game should be admitted. Players also hate to work for a coach who doesn't have the full backing of the club management.

Ned Harkness had many things going for him as a college coach. To have allowed him to be successful in professional hockey also would have meant giving success to an outsider. Hockey players and even club owners are afraid of outsiders. They are afraid of shocks.

When I came to the Flyers in 1971, I was not an outsider. My professional credentials extended over twenty-five years. I was hardly a shock to management or the players. Fortunately, I didn't suffer from Ned's problems.

But I had my own peculiar problems. Never having coached a National Hockey League team before, I began to doubt my capabilities as a coach for the Flyers. Would I be able to do a good job? How long would it last? Would these young fellows be receptive to my ideas? Would they train and play without questioning my methods? How would management accept me if the methods didn't produce results for a few years? I was insecure.

A coach's function is quite simple. But putting his players through the new techniques and ideas can turn his hair gray. To instill confidence and courage, a coach goes about often beating his breast and always threatening somebody. I have tried that approach before, but after nearly fifteen years of coaching, I have come to realize that a pep talk has little value. A word of encouragement is one thing, but threats are quite useless.

My first pep talk to the Flyers ended up a dismal failure. We were in Minnesota for a game, and the Flyers' general manager, Keith Allen, found out that I was going to talk to the boys. So he decided to sit in and I decided this was my chance to show management what a dynamic coach I was. My problem was that I was so insecure, I still felt the need to prove myself.

My lecture began mildly, but before long I had worked myself into a frenzy. I didn't like the way they were playing and I even threatened to quit if the Flyers didn't win the game that night.

After my talk, Keith took me aside and told me that I didn't have to talk about quitting and that it was useless to threaten players.

"Fred, you're our coach," he said, "and you don't have to worry about losing your job if the players lose tonight. I know what it's like to reach the young fellows. Sometimes it's difficult. We're all under strain, but this is no way to win games."

Keith was right: that was no way to win games. I don't threaten my boys anymore and, instead of pep talks, I have developed a system that gives them a feeling of confidence and courage. I have been able to accomplish this because the Flyers' management is behind me.

Most hockey coaches, however, don't have that advantage. I have suffered from that disadvantage during most of my years as a coach. General managers and scouts have had the gall to tell me who should be benched and who should be on the ice.

This is a problem in hockey today. Scouts feel that in order to earn their salary, they have to tell the coach what to do. There have been instances of scouts coming up to me during the periods and telling me what I was doing wrong. Such advice confuses a coach to a point where he actually loses his grasp of the game in progress and begins to doubt himself.

I will not listen to management or scouts during the periods of any game. But I will listen to them after the game. In fact, I am one of the few coaches in the NHL who is willing to try out new methods to create a better hockey player.

It is easy for coaches to become stagnant from the same daily routine. Usually there is nothing new left for him to do. The coach's staleness often passes on to the players. A few of us who try to change the daily routine may be lucky enough to have players and management who are willing to try.

I find myself getting stale once in a while and I have to search for new plays and new practice methods to keep the Flyers interested. The Russians have done a considerable amount of research already on building a super hockey player, and I am not talking about science fiction. It's no secret what they have done with psychiatrists and physical education teachers, with electrolysis and blood transfusions. But will the clubs in this country do something to experiment with new methods? Surely, our methods won't be as drastic as the Russian methods.

Not so long as management is telling the coach who should be benched and who should be on the ice.

I want to be left alone when a crucial game is in progress, and to a coach every game is crucial. A coach doesn't like his train of thought disturbed, and nobody in management has the right to come to a coach or his assistants and point out his mistakes. Management must give the coach credit for his decisions, although his actions may appear strange.

For instance, early in the season I'll give certain players more ice-time because they need it to improve their game and understand the system. I also know that by giving them more ice-time we will lose some games. To get them to perform according to our system, the players must work with the others on the team during actual games. In the long run, therefore, we may lose games early in the season, but we will win later games with the same players. I have to take chances with them early in the season if I expect them to perform in the future.

When Barry Ashbee was eliminated from the playoffs last year with a nasty eye injury, I was able to put in Tom Bladon to fill the defense spot. He came through for us because I had given him plenty of ice-time during the year. If I had neglected to play Bladon, he would have lost his confidence. The pressure of Stanley Cup hockey would have destroyed him and the team's chances of winning.

chapter 8

Inside the Flyers' System

In the last thirty years, since the beginning of the red line, we have done nothing in center ice. Every other team does the same thing: they get the puck over to the center; if the wings are covered, they shoot it in. The Russians have advanced beyond that stage already. Instead of shooting the puck, they will create openings. I picked up this technique from the Russians, and ours is the only team in the NHL that has been using this method of play.

For instance, Bobby Clarke has the puck at center ice, but our wings are covered. Let's say all the centers are lefthanded this year. Say Leach breaks away from his wing and heads for the defenseman to create an opening. But Bobby Clarke can't move the puck to Leach, because the wing is shadowing Leach. Bobby automatically moves to the right side and, since he is lefthanded, he'll stick-handle better and fake better. When he gets into shooting position, Bobby will be shooting at more net. Now it so happens that nobody is watching Bill Barber on the left side. Then it is his job to cut to the middle and Bobby will hit him with a pass. If he doesn't get the pass to Barber, then he immediately cuts to the outside of Barber to create an opening.

The Russians are creating openings even in their own zone. They will weave and cut to get away from the wings and create openings.

The Russians are also using long passes. But I am against long passes. I believe in the fifteen-foot pass at all times, because I believe in as little skating as possible. I don't want to skate an inch further than I have to in our system. But this is contrary to the Russian technique. They are always in motion.

My system demands economy of motion. We don't have to beat anyone to pass the puck. We don't believe in carrying the puck. To us, the name of the game is passing.

But then there are a few superstars, like Bobby Orr of the Boston Bruins and Brad Park of the Rangers, who have to show their ability at stick-handling to the fans. All they are doing is wasting time. Superstars always try to beat the system. They have to prove that they are above any system their coaches or the game can develop. That's the problem with the game today. Look at Boston: they are behind in their standings. Has all that fancy handing by Orr given them any supremacy in the league this year? Hockey is not a one-man show, it is a team sport. By showing off to the fans, these superstars are always tired by the time the third period comes around.

So, we will do one of two things when we are playing Boston. We'll give Orr the puck and let him play with it, which he is bound to do because he is such a showman. Before long he is going to tire and, as he tires out, he will become less effective. The second alternative is to double team him; by that I mean putting two on one, leaning heavily on him so he can't make a breakaway.

With my system, we must outnumber the opposition in every zone and in every situation. In other words, if Van Impe has the puck in our zone and the opposition has two men in our zone, we must have three.

Only one man leaves our zone at any time.

He could be a centerman or a wing, and he leaves the zone to create an opening.

Quite often, in professional hockey, the defenseman has the puck, but all of a sudden there is no one to pass to because he is left alone in his zone. Possibly his wingman has gone into a turn and he cannot pass the puck to him till he comes out of the turn. As the wingman or center goes to take a position along the boards or center ice, his back is turned toward the defense. In such a case, the defenseman has to go behind the net and then come out.

In our system, nobody turns his back at any time, nobody leaves a man stranded in any zone and no more than one man leaves the zone to create an opening.

Switching wings is another technique that the Russians use effectively; so do the Flyers. In 1974, we won a crucial game against the Montreal Canadiens in Philadelphia. They were beating us 4–2 and 8 minutes were left in the third period. Expecting the Flyers to lose that game, the fans had started to leave the Spectrum.

I told my boys to switch wings every minute, and even the defensemen changed sides. Our game picked up momentum and we scored 3 goals in the last eight minutes and won the game. All the goals came from the opposite sides. We even switched the guys in the lineup during the faceoff.

Switching is not easy on a player if he is not used to it. Instead of shooting at the net from the right side, for instance, he will now have to shoot from the left side. When I first started switching players from left to right, some of the boys were upset. One said he couldn't do it. I told him, he either does what I want him to do or he gets another job. Eventually, this boy made the switch and he had the best year in his hockey career—so much so that he didn't want to go back to his original position. He had become a better hockey player in the new position and he had begun to score goals.

But just switching from left to right does not guarantee goals. Shooting the puck from the correct distance is critical in hockey, otherwise the player is merely giving the puck to the goalie. The Flyers don't have the right to shoot the puck on the net from outside the blue line, which is silly, because they are just dumping it and losing control of the puck.

I want to know where we are shooting from and why, and I don't want any shot from a distance greater than thirty feet. I like the puck handler to move in before he shoots. Sometimes we won't even take a shot on a power play, if we can't get close enough.

Everybody in hockey thinks that they have to shoot regardless of the distance. On some teams, the standing order is to shoot when the other team is short-handed two men, instead of moving the puck in close and trying to score.

When we are short-handed, we will use six units to kill penalties, whereas other teams usually have two men to kill penalties. Our units will be on the ice for no more than one minute. Even in a power play situation, each Flyers' line is allowed no more than one minute to be on the ice, and during that one minute I want an all-out effort.

This all-out effort creates the tempo of the game, whereby we are always pushing the other team, keeping them guessing as to our next move. Our tempo keeps us on the offensive and forces the opposition to make mistakes. We built up such a tempo in our game against the Bruins in Boston during the 1974 Stanley Cup playoffs that it just destroyed them.

A team cannot create the tempo of the game with just one line. Some coaches will try to favor one line over the others, thereby giving the other lines a sense of inferiority. I can put Kindrachuk's line against Esposito's line and not worry about it, because our lines are all good and are capable of playing against any line in professional hockey today.

Boston will play the Esposito line for a 4-minute shift, while we'll have three lines against them in that time. Thus, by moving our lines on a 1-minute shift, we can create a faster tempo during the game. We don't tire as much as the opposition, and we always have a fresh player on the ice.

Since we change our lines more often than the other teams do to maintain the tempo of the game, every line has to put out 100 percent on the ice. They cannot slouch around or play defensively and wait for chances to occur, because they are going to be changed quickly. Therefore, they have to play offensively and create openings and their own chances. They can do this if they commit themselves completely for the time they are on the ice.

Complete commitment means we go after the goals. It hurts a line's performance if a coach tells him just to keep the play going without trying to be offensive. In effect, he is telling him that he is not good enough to play. This type of thinking destroys his confidence.

Another common practice among hockey coaches is to tell the players to watch the opponent's superstar. All hockey players have been brought up with that attitude, and it is very much a traditional part of the game. I had done that during my early years as a coach, but no more will I tell my players to watch an Orr or Esposito. We don't even mention their names.

I'll never forget the first time the Flyers played Bobby Hull of the Chicago Black Hawks. Being new at coaching an NHL team, I told my team to watch Hull and put one man on him all the time, and he did a pretty good job of watching Hull.

But Bobby Hull is one of the greatest players that the game has ever produced and he knew what we were doing. He is also one of the strongest guys around. I am told that he picks up big bales of hay weighing 250 pounds with a pitchfork and heaves them around like they were cushions.

Well, that night he destroyed our lines, because we just couldn't tire him out. It was late in the game and the score was tied 0–0. Suddenly, he got the puck for a fraction of a second at center ice. Now my man was with him, but Hull flicked one of his famous wrist shots and scored. Obviously, we had relied too much on the traditional system of watching him rather than taking the play away from him.

That's when I made up my mind never to watch a man again. Maurice (Rocket) Richard was another great player, who was always watched by the opposition. For fifteen years they trailed him constantly; in spite of being watched, he scored goal after goal. Richard also scored most of his goals from fifteen to twenty feet. He would also switch sides and confuse the defensemen and the goalie.

Rocket Richard was a superb skater, no doubt, and so were all the early players on the

Montreal Canadiens team. They literally outskated the other teams without consciously realizing that they were better skaters than most of the opposition. They were always considered a skating club, not a hitting club. They skated 2- and 3-minute shifts, because that was the traditional way of playing hockey.

If they had changed their lines more often, they would have been a really superb hockey club. They had the speed and the tempo because they had the players, but their lines stayed on the ice too long. Jean Beliveau, for instance, might be out there on the ice for 3 minutes, skating like mad and tiring himself.

The Russians believe in five-man units and all working together. Every man knows exactly what the other man is going to do in every situation. When I played defense and our center had the puck, I had no idea what he was going to do. In a typical game, the wings may have had some idea of what the center was going to do, but generally, we never worked as a five-man unit.

For instance, the left winger would have the puck deep in the corner, and I could stand free all night and never get the puck. He was going to do what he wanted, and nobody knew what he was going to do, not even the coach. But the Russians don't play that way and neither do the Flyers.

We have developed many plays that we work on constantly. We know where everybody is supposed to be at all times. We also talk to each other on the ice. The center doesn't have time to look around and see who is open. Clarke's right wing will say he is open or the defenseman will say, "don't pass to him because he is still covered." If the spectators are making a lot of noise and we can't hear each other, we will tap the ice to communicate. Most hockey players don't talk often enough on the ice.

chapter 9

What's the Future for Hockey?

In this country, the game of hockey is still in its infancy. We have a lot to learn from the European and the Russian systems. Even the Japanese are coming on strong. With their desire to excel and ability to follow directions, the Japanese will make formidable hockey players.

The government of the People's Republic of China has also shown interest in the game;

one of the NHL officials was over there last year at their invitation.

Evidently, if we are going to be the best, we have to change a lot of things in hockey. Let's start with the rink. Today's rinks are small and too confining for good stick handlers. In a bigger rink, a poor player will not survive because he will not be able to catch up with the better skaters. The roughhouse skaters, therefore, will be left behind. Defensemen can't be bulls in a bigger rink. They will have to develop finesse and make the moves. In smaller rinks, a mediocre player is able to cover up his mistakes.

All rinks in the league today are not the same size; I have noticed that better skaters always have difficulty in the smaller rinks. In effect, the rinks should be, on the average, at least five feet wider.

But like everything else in hockey, changes occur very slowly. We haven't gotten over our fear of outsiders, even though these outsiders and their techniques may be helpful to the team. Periodically, such outsiders as psychologists and psychiatrists have helped players. But their value is not fully recognized by hockey clubs.

Management will spend a lot of money to get a team out of its depression. They might even consent to bring in a management expert. He might as well be a witch doctor from Africa, because nobody is going to listen to him.

But if a motivational expert wants to teach me something, I am willing to listen. In fact, I will listen to any expert who can help make the Flyers the best team in hockey. Big corporations use motivational experts to give confidence to their staff. Why can't we use the same techniques in professional hockey?

Professional baseball teams have trainers on their staff. But there are no such positions in hockey. We don't even listen to physical education teachers who can develop a new set of exercises or drills for hockey players. Most hockey players fall back on the old standby, lifting weights. But muscle alone is not enough. Good hockey also requires brains.

Even when new techniques are brought to the game, the coaches shouldn't expect to see results overnight. Instead, they should expect resistance from their players. It is not fair to blame hockey players for being cautious about team activities. Strange as it may seem, most hockey players have developed a habit of working alone, and it takes some time to break that pattern. The reason they have developed this habit is because they never had a system to guide them. The coaches just left them to their own devices. When I played for the New York Rangers, lacing your skates and skating were considered enough. We did no calisthenics, had no obstacle courses or series of plays to run through. There was a general belief that skating was the best exercise and scrimmages the best conditioners.

Coaches have to develop new plays and drills to keep the players interested. A coach who is willing to learn new techniques anywhere he can find them will eventually develop a system for his players. There is enough material in our medical and psychology books about the human body and mind. We must learn how it works and how to bring out the best without destroying the individual.

Coaches should learn from other sports. For instance, the concept of the five-man unit's total involvement came from soccer and basketball. Hockey always had five-man units, but they all worked as five separate one-man units.

Briefly, therefore, the first requirement is the five-man total involvement.

Second, the team must be able to counter check aggressively at all times, and attack with speed and take the offensive.

Physical conditioning of the players to develop strength, speed and agility is the third criterion.

Fourth, players must create openings and initiate plays.

Fifth, they must be able to spot the opposition's weak areas and take advantage of them by forcing plays that will put the other team on the defensive.

Players must make the puck do the work by maximizing their passing skills, is the sixth requirement.

Seventh, develop puck control not only with the stick, but also with the feet.

Eighth, get ready to play with a positive frame of mind.

Ninth, a positive attitude is only possible if the team has developed superior plays and everyone on the team knows what these plays are.

Tenth, all this requires a lot of discipline.

Hockey is the fastest game that a man on two feet can play.

chapter 10
Predictably Unpredictable

Motivation takes many forms, but regardless of the specifics it has to be positive. When I first started coaching, I tried all the traditional methods of motivating my players. I'd put up on the board all the rotten things the opposition had said about us. Most coaches do that. The idea, of course, is to get the players mad enough to hate the opposition. But that doesn't work with professional athletes. It's a childish method that's good for kids. Now, I personally don't care what the opposition thinks of us, and I don't want to win games by calling our opposition all kinds of names. Besides, the Flyers don't need that rah-rah type of motivation one finds in the dressing rooms of many other hockey teams.

The morning after a game, we have a workout and then we go over our entire system. Repetition is the best method. I might bring one or two players to my office and discuss the previous day's game and their performance. I will begin the discussion by talking about their good points. I will tell them how well they have played in the past, how good they are and how much we need them.

Then I will zero in on the things that they are doing wrong. I will try to hit the one sore spot about which I am upset. I will tell them I am upset about their performance regarding that particular play, because I know they can improve it. So when the players leave my office, they are in a good frame of mind. They feel that it is just one thing that needs improvement in relation to all the other good things that they are doing.

I try to harp on the positive aspects of the game as much as possible. I will hit the negative aspect lightly, but I know it will register. These are intelligent boys, and they are also very sensitive. Therefore, I can't overdo the negative aspect. If they were not good enough, they wouldn't be in the league. Obviously, they are all good, but not to the same degree. If I were to harp on the negative aspects of their game and bear down on them continuously about their weaknesses every day, day in and day out, these boys would go crazy and wouldn't have any confidence in themselves.

Take the second game against the Islanders in the 1975 semifinals in Philadelphia before the Stanley Cup Championship. I didn't know that Parent wasn't going to make it. There was only five minutes to go and I had to put him in my lineup. I didn't even know that he was hurt. I walked into the dressing room, gave the boys a quick talk and noticed Bernie in the trainer's room. That was the first time I knew that he was hurt. I immediately walked out of the trainer's room without saying a word to him and went down the game's lineup.

"Stephenson, Van Impe, Jimmy Watson...."

The worst thing I could have done was to show visible concern for Bernie. Certainly I was worried, but I didn't have to show the whole world that I was worried by moping around. I would have merely succeeded in creating fear and concern in the minds of the others on the team.

I talked to the team as if the loss of Bernie for that game were no problem. We have seventeen men plus two goalies, and they are a team. No one man is the team. Everyone has his work cut out for him. He has to skate, check, block and do the job assigned to him in his zone.

Another coach in this position, with Bernie out of the lineup, would have said: "Well now our best goalie is not there, so we better double up our efforts or we'll lose the game. Stephenson hasn't played in months. OK men, let's go, let's win this one for Bernie."

That kind of talk is for motivating kids, not professional athletes. Stephenson became my regular goalie and I emphasized that fact by being normal about it. Of course, there was no reason to behave any other way.

But if I had taken him aside and told him not to be nervous and take it easy, we'll try to protect you, I would have created a crisis situation. That type of cautious behavior would have clearly indicated that I didn't have confidence in him. It would have been the worst thing for me to have said: "Look men, Stephenson hasn't played in months, so let's watch him and give him protection."

If I had said that, I would have destroyed the whole system. As far as I was concerned, putting Stephenson in was the most normal thing to do. I maintained that feeling by putting him in the lineup without a fuss, and nobody on the team raised any doubts about his abilities.

By being normal, I motivated Stephenson. I

showed confidence in his capabilities as a professional and treated him like an adult. If I had treated him like a kid, I would have expected a childish reaction not only from Stephenson but from the entire team. They wouldn't have played their regular game; they would have become overly cautious and defensive.

So we all pretended that there was no crisis.

Successful coaches who have helped me through my years as a player always emphasized the positive aspects. They knew when to pat a guy on the back and when to kick him in the rear end when the job wasn't done—but not in front of the other players. Some kicks have to be given in the privacy of a coach's office.

Occasionally a player will come over and say, "Fred, I didn't want to tell you this, but my knee is sore." So I tell him not to worry, that I'll spot him here and there, and put him on the ice for short spurts only. But generally, they want encouragement from me. They want me to know that they may not be at their best, but they don't want anybody else to know. But at times, when we are playing a big game, some players will want out. There are a lot of athletes who are afraid of playing in big games, and they will suddenly develop pains and hurts. I guess one could call them psychosomatic. The game is crucial, with five minutes left, and the player will want me to put someone in his place because his leg is bothering him. In many cases, the leg may be bothering him and the player might feel that his performance will be affected. But I would never pull that player out, unless he is badly hurt.

I will not try to favor any player, instead I will make him play. I have found through the years that a player needs an extra push. He wants to play, but he needs a vote of confidence. He looks to me for encouragement. He is questioning his performance and wants assurance from me that he will be OK. Maybe another player could do a better job, but I want him—not the other guy—on the ice. I want to keep that rotation going. I can't tell players why I am doing something. I can't tell one that he is not as tough as the other guy. That will destroy him. I have my reasons for putting certain players on the ice even in a crucial game.

I know my personnel. I know who to humor and who will not be humored. The players are all individuals; they have the right to be different. Therefore, they can't all be treated the same. Some are more sensitive than others, some are more intelligent and some are more hardworking than others. The coach who tries to handle his players the same way is not successful for long.

The morning before every game, we will have a meeting for not more than ten minutes. I don't believe in dragging out a meeting. During the meeting I will inject some new ideas. But they are not necessarily new in the sense of brand new. It could be a new play or a new move, something they heard a couple of days or weeks before.

"I've gone over my system a couple of thousand times. Does anybody want me to go over it again?" I said one morning.

"Oh, please, not again," came the cries from the team.

"Does that mean we know it all?"

And Joe Watson shouts, "Oh yeah, oh yeah, we know it all."

"Thank god, somebody knows it all. Even I don't know it all, because I've some doubts. We'll let the system go till tonight when I'll go over some points with you. But for now, let's go over this new team we are facing. Let's discuss all their weaknesses. If you know of any, let me know."

Bobby Clarke came up with some suggestions that I didn't know before. Then Gary Dornhoefer, the seasoned veteran, came up with a few, and before long just about everybody had something to say. Obviously they had done their homework and spotted their opposition just as well as their coaching staff.

This is one way of motivating players. They can't help but put out their best effort on the ice because they are putting their best effort forth during the discussions. They are making a contribution to the game whether they are on the ice or in the dressing room or drinking beer.

During our discussions, I try to hammer all the little details into their minds. "If we ever get home free," I told the team before the semifinal game in 1975 against the Islanders, "we'll be able to score by going to their goalie's right or left because he comes out too far. He is out so far, don't shoot. Shoot the second shot up high, because he doesn't get up fast enough. Think, he is down, shoot up. He is down, shoot up."

That's how MacLeish scored the goal—by shooting up. The man was already down before the shot came. So I have to keep reminding them about all these little details, and they just might remember the instructions at the right time.

Part of motivation is injecting humor and fun into the talk. Joe Watson likes to make jokes. He will pretend that he doesn't like the attention, but he does enjoy being center stage.

Bernie came in the other day and he was mad at me. He said: "I read in the paper what you said about my $500 bed. My wife was really mad. She says, 'The pillows are worth $500, and nobody sleeps in a cheap bed like that.'"

So everybody had a laugh. I told him, "My wife and I have these two army cots, and I'm always falling between the cracks." So we laughed again.

But when all the laughing is done, we get down to business. But you've got to inject humor, and they even try to make fun of me. Sometimes I will pretend that I'm dumb, and they will all try to help me as if I were not the smartest guy in the world. There were a few minutes to go in the second period against the Islanders, and we had a man in the box. I said, Van Impe goes with Joe Watson, and with Clarke, Leach and Lonsberry. Oh, the guys on the bench were in an uproar. They were trying to tell me that Van Impe was still in the penalty box. I had pretended that I didn't know. Sometimes we have double penalties and I may try to figure out how much time is still left, but the boys will tell me, "Don't worry, we'll figure it out."

The point is, everybody on the team is participating in all aspects of the game whether they are sitting on the bench or playing on the ice. They are also helping me with my lapses of memory. But I am not doing this for fun, I am testing them. I want to see if they are really interested in the game, in the team and in me. They know the system so well by now that they are all acting like coaches.

For instance, if I say "wings on wings," and if the player is not on wings they will jump up and tell him. I don't have to tell them all the time what to do. They are telling and instructing each other.

Well, three minutes are left in the period and the score is pretty close, so I'll say, "Van Impe and Jimmy Watson." I know I don't want Van Impe and Watson together. The guys will immediately say, "Freddy, put Bladon in, he's good at the point." OK, I'll say, thanks for reminding me. I have to get them wrapped up in the game so they feel they are helping me coach the team. They are not just sitting on the bench like animals waiting for their turn to get on the ice.

We are all involved and not afraid to say anything to each other. For instance, a player will come to me and say, "Freddy, you're working so and so too hard." I know I'm working him hard, and I know he is five pounds overweight. These players are concerned for each other.

But on our team, we are not afraid to correct the coach or even a star player like Bobby Clarke. If Bobby doesn't follow the system or makes a mistake, the players will be on him even before I can get to him. They will tell Bobby that he was taking chances, or that he broke away from the system.

The system comes first. It is above superstars, and it has to be followed to the letter, even by Clarke, Leach or MacLeish or the other players. Otherwise, a team might be just a bunch of boys who are out there doing whatever comes into their heads.

In my days, Lindsay, Abel and Howe were the best line in hockey. Lindsay was the right winger. Abel was the center and Howe was just a rookie and on left wing. That line functioned as a unit. They did things according to their leader, Mr. Abel. The three of them had worked out their plays and knew what they were doing. But that wasn't enough, because their defensemen didn't know what was on their minds. The defense was left out, which is wrong. Their system was incomplete because it wasn't a five-man unit working together.

Also in those days, and even today, each forward line had a different system. Not so with the Flyers. Each line must do the same thing. They must follow the pattern. In my days as a player, the forwards did what they wanted, the defensemen did as they pleased and the coach hoped that we were right. The Flyers are the only team with a system in every zone.

That's what I don't like about superstars in hockey. I believe that the best player on the team, no matter how talented he is, must conform to the system. I don't like him to break away from the system—not even to score a goal. If he breaks away from the system, then everybody is going to break away from it. I don't believe in setting up special situations just for this particular talent.

However, I'll do this. In the same game

against the Islanders, I put our best scorers on the front line, Clarke, our man in the middle, MacLeish and Leach.

I told them, "Once we get the puck deep in their zone, I want MacLeish to take the faceoff. You're pretty good at faceoffs. I want Clarke to take the wing if the puck goes in the corner. You're a better man in the corner."

Clarke thinks fast in the corner, while MacLeish is the right guy in the circle within a good scoring position, and he also had that quick shot. Leach is in front of the nets ready to deflect the puck. So in three seconds we scored a goal.

I made these changes to use the best talent in the right spots. I know that I can manipulate my superstars and they will do exactly as they are supposed to and not do their own thing. For a long time, I have used Bobby to take the faceoff with MacLeish in the corner. But I have found that MacLeish has the talent to be in the middle. Bobby is good at holding the puck in the corner and faking the opposition.

But in the case of superstars like Park and Orr, they seem to do what they want to do anytime, which is not good for the team. And possibly, the reason they get away with it is because the coach is afraid to say anything. Maybe he is hoping they made the right decision. The superstars take the gamble and hope it pays off.

On our team, Bobby Clarke is a big motivational factor. He is the only true athlete I have seen in modern sports. He will give up his goals and assists for the team. He's not as interested in his own records as other superstars are, he's not obsessed with scoring the most points or goals. The things he does for the team are unbelievable.

For instance, he will say to me, "I want Kelly with me today. You are not using him much and he hasn't had a goal for a long time. He needs some points to get confidence. Just let me have him for a few shifts. Maybe I can give him some help and get him a point or two, maybe he'll play better."

Here is Bobby Clarke, the superstar of the Flyers and one of the most talked about players in hockey history, and he's going to sacrifice his career for a while for that individual, even though he knows that he will not get the points to be up on the scoring list.

One day I found the players working out some business deal, and Barry Ashbee said that he isn't anything any more. Clarke immediately jumped up and said, "What do you mean you're nothing, you're one of us. We're all going to share in this equally." Then he says we should get the trainers in on this thing.

Someone said, "Who needs the trainers?"

Clarke jumps again: "What did you say? What do you mean, who needs the trainers? They are part of the team also. We'll all make money together."

Now Bobby Clarke doesn't need all this hassle. Just on the strength of his fame, he can make money for everybody, but he is for the team and not for himself.

Andre Dupont is not yet a superstar. He was just a kid when I had him in his second year in professional hockey. He was wild and overly aggressive. Finally, when I realized we could get him in a trade with St. Louis rather cheaply, I couldn't believe it. He was all raw talent.

He is one of the few athletes who will say openly that he's not the brightest guy around and needs help. He is not ashamed to ask questions. He wants to get better all the time. And although he has established himself as a good hockey player, he comes to me more than anybody else on the team. I have given him all the books on hockey that I have, and he has read them all. Even during the course of the game, if he does something wrong, he will start asking questions. And I have to say, "Andre, please, if you did something wrong, tell me about it between the periods, not now." It's hard for him to explain exactly what happened. So between periods he will draw the positions on the blackboard and explain to me what he did wrong.

Dupont is the most inquisitive player I have ever coached, but sometimes he can be too inquisitive. Well, he says, someday maybe he will coach, and I think he will make a good one. He is not the know-it-all type, like some guys. But I won't give him any favorable treatment. I will answer all his questions, and I will answer questions from any other player. I will not play favorites. Not even with Parent.

Bernie walked in with a swollen neck the other day, while I was busy in the office. He was looking for sympathy. I fired back: "What do you want me to do? I'm not the doctor. Go see the doctor."

Bernie's the greatest goalie in the NHL today, but he will get the same treatment from me that Dupont, or any others will get.

Victory, or at least the taste of it, can do strange things to a coach. And there is nothing sweeter than the Stanley Cup Championship. But before we could get to drink from that cup, so to speak, our path led us through Boston, its boisterous fans and the star-studded Bruins. It was our last game in Boston, and we had to win that one to even out the series in the finals of the playoffs in 1974. But the Bruins fans had decided that we were not to have our way. They had already pelted our bus with eggs and when we arrived at the arena they were waiting for us. It was as if we were the Christians who were shortly to be fed to the bruising, brawny, pompous Bruin lions, and the crowd had assembled to see the massacre.

We were the underdogs and we were supposed to cower and scrape our tails and bow to the team that had already made predictions of a victory. Well, if statistics were enough to predict the future, the Flyers were destined for defeat, because we had not won a single game against the Bruins in Boston in a long while. The reporters had already picked the winners.

But the Flyers had scored the goal in the first period and kept the Bruins away all through the first, second and even the third period. I looked up at the clock and the period still had about three minutes to go. I clutched the rosary in my right hand as tightly as I could, and suddenly I felt as if I would faint. All the pressures of the playoffs began to bear down on me and the medication I was taking made it worse.

Just before the playoffs had started, I had fallen on the ice and wrenched my chest muscles. I tried to put off going to the doctor but the constant worry about the upcoming games and the pain in my chest kept me awake most nights. Finally, my wife Marietta couldn't take it any longer so I went to our doctor, hoping to get some relief. Instead, the good doctor told me the pain in my chest would eventually subside.

For relief he gave me sleeping pills so I could get some rest. The pills not only made me sleepy but their effect lingered on during the daytime and made me groggy.

As I stood behind the Flyers bench in Boston, my mind began to wander. My fifteen years of coaching life flashed before me, and now I had the opportunity of reaching the top of my career as the coach of the Stanley Cup Champions. But I knew anything could happen in three minutes. One goal lead was not enough to give any coach a comfortable feeling. I tried to keep my best men on the ice. But suddenly I wanted to give everybody a chance to be part of the game. I wanted to give this guy a break and that guy a break. But I shouldn't have done that. I should have been strong and resisted my impulses. I remember Terry Crisp changing my mind four or five times. He would give me a few dirty looks because he knew that I shouldn't be sending guys on the ice who were not strong enough.

He said something to the effect that this was no time to fool around, getting sentimental about giving guys breaks. I couldn't believe that in a crucial game like that I could suddenly turn soft.

I had these fellows with me for over a year, and I thought maybe I could get by with one more shift. I knew deep down that they shouldn't be out there, and at the same time I was hoping that nothing would go wrong. I should have used only the seven or eight best guys we had on the team for the last three minutes. I finally jolted myself from that strange feeling. I could feel the rosary cutting into the skin of my palm. By now the Flyers had managed to hold onto the lead; when the final buzzer sounded, I suddenly felt empty.

As a coach I've always been difficult to understand because coaching is not all that cut and dried. Players don't know why I'm holding back one player for a few games, and then when I put him back into the game, he suddenly begins to score the goals. I have my reasons for doing these things. Why did America buy Alaska 100 years ago? Did they know there was oil? Maybe it was bought on a hunch, or maybe it was a political move to put a buffer zone between Russia and the Western hemisphere.

Everything must be new and different. For instance, imagine we just won a game by three goals. Everyone thinks he did well. Now that's the time to shock the team. I know coaches who would say, "Wonderful, keep it up."

I don't have to tell them that they are doing well when they win a game. They already know it. When they are winning, that is the time to tell them about their mistakes. They are more receptive then because it has a shock value. This technique of mine might have created the impression that I am unpredictable.

For instance, say Gary Dornhoefer scored a couple of beautiful goals, and he is all happy about it. Now he is looking for a third one, and he might momentarily forget about the rhythm of the system because he is happy. He might not think defensively. All these aspects of the player's personality and the nature of the game have to be considered before I shock him.

Between periods, I will try to find something that's truly wrong with his plays and point out the mistakes he made. I'm mad now, or at least I'm pretending to be mad. Gary, or whoever it is I'm giving hell, will probably say to himself, "What's the matter with Freddy? Here I scored some beautiful goals, and he is chewing my ass out. I just can't figure him out."

It isn't so much that I am hard on Gary or Lonsberry, but I want the others on the team to hear me. I want them to know that just because he scored two goals, everything is not just OK. There are a number of other things he did wrong, and maybe he was lucky. This is one way of bringing them down to earth.

I will also make changes during the game or just before the game, which may make my behavior seem unpredictable. In 1975, against the Islanders, I switched Schultz and Saleski. I will occasionally change my strategy without even knowing ahead of time myself. It depends on what the opposition is doing. The changes I make are not that different because I've made those changes during the course of the year when we played other teams. So when I make changes, the players know what to do. Sometimes when we are leading by a comfortable margin, I will make changes to see how the players accept the changes, because in the future we may have to do that in a crucial game. So the changes are made under game conditions and the players know how to handle themselves.

The other day, which was the first time in a month I had Saleski and Schultz switch wings, I didn't tell them until game time. I don't like to worry them. I know they can do it because they have done it in practice and during other games. Again, when they do something different like that, they have to concentrate more on the game and do things right. I don't want them to know why I switched wings. They know it is good for the game and they will do it. I wanted Schultz against the opposition's tough man, and Saleski against their good checker. Saleski is a better checker than Schultz.

When we return to the lockerroom between periods, I write down everything that we did wrong or weaknesses of the other team or things that we should watch out for during the next period. Then, two minutes before we are ready to go on the ice, I'll tell my players the good points and the bad points and point out the number of things they can improve on.

After I instruct the team and before the buzzer sounds, I'll come out of the dressing room first and walk about aimlessly, usually lost in my thoughts. I'm so wrapped up in the game that I often walk along the corridor. Once, while we were playing an away game, I just kept walking down the corridor—before I realized what had happened, I was out of the arena and walking down the parking lot.

I couldn't get back into the arena because the doors were locked from the inside. Later, the players made fun of me and we all had a big laugh. Ed Snider was pulling his hair. He sent his men to look for me, but they never figured that I was outside the arena trying to get in. I felt lost because I'd even forgotten what city we were in. Well, finally, they found me outside, waiting patiently.

I have waited patiently all these years to make some meaningful contribution to the game of hockey. The Flyers have helped me revolutionize the game. Yet, they can't figure me out. Perhaps I'm like a father or a teacher to them. How many times can children figure out what's going through their parents' minds? I couldn't figure out what my Dad was thinking. I questioned him in my own mind. As a coach, I'm looking at the team's performance today, tomorrow and in the future. I have to consider the interests of nineteen fellows on the team, their wives and children. I love everybody, I'm hard on everybody, I will joke with them, drink beer with them, I'm one of the boys, yet I'm not one of the boys.

I'm the extension of their fathers and their big brothers whom they need when they are in trouble, when they want help, when they need protection. My door is always open when they want to come in and tell me their problems, or even to tell me that I'm full of horse manure. Call me predictably unpredictable.

Coaching Chart

Fred Shero, Flyers' Coach

Born: October 23, 1925; Winnipeg, Manitoba. Playing Height: 5'10"; Weight, 175 lb. Position: Left defense.
NHL Club: New York Rangers (1947-48; 48-49; 49-50).

PLAYING RECORD

Year	Team	League	GP	Regular Schedule G	A	PTS	PIM	GP	Playoffs G	A	PTS	PIM
1946-47	New Haven	AHL	3	0	0	0	6	—	—	—	—	—
1947-48	St. Paul	USHL	40	9	14	23	20	—	—	—	—	—
1947-48	New York	NHL	19	1	0	1	2	6	0	1	1	6
1948-49	New York	NHL	59	3	6	9	64	—	—	—	—	—
1949-50	New York	NHL	67	2	8	10	71	7	0	1	1	2
1949-50	New Haven	AHL	2	1	0	1	0	—	—	—	—	—
1950-51	Cincinnati	AHL	65	5	17	22	94	—	—	—	—	—
1951-52	Cleveland	AHL	15	2	2	4	10	3	0	1	1	2
1951-52	Seattle	PCHL	43	1	16	17	46	—	—	—	—	—
1952-53	Cleveland	AHL	64	4	14	18	54	9	2	1	3	16
1953-54	Cleveland	AHL	69	21	32	53	95	9	2	3	5	16
1954-55	Cleveland	AHL	37	8	14	22	54	—	—	—	—	—
1955-56	Winnipeg	WHL	59	8	24	32	99	6	0	2	2	8
1956-57	Winnipeg	WHL	66	8	24	32	52	—	—	—	—	—
1957-58	Shawinigan	QPHL	48	1	5	6	50	4	0	1	1	10
	NHL TOTALS		145	6	14	20	137	13	0	2	2	8
	TOTALS		656	74	176	250	717	44	4	12	16	60

COACHING RECORD

Year	Team	League	W	L	T	PTS	GF	GA	Place of Finish
1957-58	Shawinigan	QPHL	31	28	5	67	243	235	2nd–Playoff Champs
1958-59	*								
1959-60	St. Paul	IHL	41	21	6	88	261	188	1st West–Playoff Champs
1960-61	St. Paul	IHL	46	22	4	96	309	233	2nd West–Playoff Champs
1961-62	St. Paul	IHL	42	25	1	85	291	209	2nd
1962-63	St. Paul	IHL	23	44	3	49	241	328	6th
1963-64	St. Paul	CPHL	38	30	4	80	259	230	2nd
1964-65	St. Paul	CPHL	41	23	6	88	281	223	1st–Playoff Champs
1965-66	Minnesota	CPHL	34	25	11	79	229	197	1st
1966-67	Omaha	CPHL	36	24	10	82	262	203	2nd
1967-68	Buffalo	AHL	32	28	12	76	239	224	3rd West
1968-69	Buffalo	AHL	41	18	15	97	282	192	1st West
1969-70	Buffalo	AHL	40	17	15	95	280	193	1st West–Playoff Champs
1970-71	Omaha	CHL	45	16	11	101	312	216	1st Playoff Champs
1971-72	FLYERS	NHL	26	38	14	66	200	236	4th West
1972-73	FLYERS	NHL	37	30	11	85	296	256	2nd West
1973-74	FLYERS	NHL	50	16	12	112	273	164	1st West–Stanley Cup Champs
1974-75	FLYERS	NHL	51	18	11	113	293	181	Division & Conference Champs†
	TOTALS		634	423	151	1459	4551	3708	

* Out of hockey.
† Stanley Cup playoffs still in progress as of publication.